THE POOR MAN'S GUIDE
TO ANTIQUE COLLECTING

THE
POOR MAN'S GUIDE
TO
ANTIQUE COLLECTING

John Mebane

DOUBLEDAY & COMPANY, INC.

Garden City, New York

1969

Library of Congress Catalog Card Number 77–84382
Copyright © 1969 by John Mebane
All Rights Reserved
Printed in the United States of America
First Edition

Contents

———————⋄———————

CONTENTS   ix

A NOTE OF THANKS

The author expresses his appreciation to the following individuals and institutions for their help in connection with the preparation of this book:

The Antiques Journal and the Babka Publishing Company for permission to draw upon material written by the author for *The Antiques Journal* and for providing illustrations.

The Atlanta Journal and *The Atlanta Constitution* for permission to draw upon material written for these newspapers.

The James B. Beam Distilling Company for photographs.

Better Homes & Gardens for permission to draw upon background researched by the author for this publication.

The Coca-Cola Company for a photograph.

Dant Distillers Company for photographs.

Clarence T. Hubbard of West Hartford, Connecticut, for permission to quote from an article by him that appeared in *The Antiques Journal.*

The National Life Insurance Company of Vermont for photographs.

The Rev. Wayne S. Nordstrom of Galva, Illinois, for a photograph.

Old Sturbridge Village of Sturbridge, Massachusetts, for photographs.

H. R. Bradley Smith and the Shelburne Museum of Shelburne, Vermont, for permission to quote from Mr. Smith's book *Blacksmiths' and Farriers' Tools at Shelburne Museum,* published by the museum, and for photographs.

Yankee magazine for permission to draw upon background researched by the author for an article appearing in that publication.

Western Collector for permission to draw upon background for an article reseached by the author for that publication.

He also expresses heartfelt appreciation to Hannah K. Mebane for permitting him to litter the dining table with manuscripts, catalogues, and assorted miscellany while engaged in the preparation of this book, thereby forcing his family to eat in the kitchen for six months.

THE POOR MAN'S GUIDE
TO ANTIQUE COLLECTING

Caviar for the Poor

———— ⬥ ————

THAT old saw to the effect that poor folks are glad of porridge has been knocked into a cocked hat by Congress in more ways than one. Our lawmakers conferred upon our impecunious hordes one of the great boons of the century when they decreed not very long ago that numerous objects need be only a century of age to be "legitimate antiques." This bit of legalistic maneuvering swept away the 1830 barrier that had theretofore existed and now permits us to embrace within the category of antiques literally thousands of articles that postdate the Civil War, the Pony Express ride between Sacramento and St. Joseph, and our acquisition of Alaska from Russia at two cents an acre.

Prior to this redefinition, "antiques" were collected largely by individuals and institutions amply endowed with legal tender. Artifacts of the eighteenth century and before were high-priced, scarce, and somewhat awesome. Today, however, the bungalow dweller and the tenant of the two-room apartment can join in the pursuit of the antique for fun and profit.

Naturally, this distresses some fastidious collectors whose acquisitions of the rare and the beautiful have been attended periodically with a bit of pomp and circumstance. It also is a burr under the saddle of certain high-minded dealers in antiquities who look with abhorrence upon the tendency to collect anything of lesser consequence than Giovanni de Bologna bronzes, fourteenth-century ivory diptychs, and Kutani porcelain. But whatever hue and cry has escaped from the anguished lips of the elite has been smothered by squeals of joy from hoi polloi now suddenly admitted to the sport of monarchs and millionaires. For collecting is a sport, and it can be a joyous one for the knowledgeable. This is a point that needs amplification.

One can lose his shirt (or her petticoat) as easily and as quickly in the pursuit of riches from antiques as one can in the pursuit of wealth from stocks and bonds if one does not know what he is doing. While it can be fun to buy trash, it does not follow that it is profitable. Consequently, all collectors—and beginning collectors in particular—need to know how to distinguish trash from potential treasure. If you intend to collect either antiques or objects that you hope will become antiques before long as an investment, you want to be reasonably certain that there will be a market for your collection in the future. If no one wants what you have amassed by laborious effort and shrewd bargaining, you may be on your way to the poorhouse.

On the other hand, if you know what you're doing, you may find antiques a better investment than many stocks and bonds. Let's not beat around the bush. It is the hope of a profit in the future that is attracting many into this business of collecting right now. Naturally, the collector should have some incentive in addition to profit, such as an appreciation of the art of her forefathers or an impelling need to grace the floor or wall space of her home with useful and/or decorative mementoes of the past. A lot of young newly married couples are actually furnishing their homes or apartments with furniture and accessories that have recently been thrust into the category of antiques or with more recent stuff they have reason to believe will become collectible within a short span of time. And some of them are saving money by so doing, because the price escalation that attends collectible objects in demand has not yet been able to overtake scores of things just beginning to move into the category of collectibles. Give it a little time, and it will.

The trouble with many beginning collectors is that they do not yet know how to distinguish the good from the bad, the desirable from the undesirable, the mink from the hamster. They sink their hard-earned cash into furniture that will never make the grade, baubles that will never attain allure, or (sometimes abetted by beginning dealers who

don't know the difference themselves) modern reproductions which they
are unable to distinguish from originals. There are also more than a
few who will buy from the antique dealers' shelves anything with
which they are unfamiliar but which seems to be reasonably priced.
Some of my friends do this, and they tell me they do so because it gives
them an opportunity to study and learn about strange objects. More
often than not, they do learn—but they learn the hard way. What they
frequently learn is that these unfamiliar objects are dogs—things nobody
wants. Especially the dealers who were trying frantically to get rid
of them.

I don't mean to cast aspersions at dealers. Most of them are honest,
hard-working, God-fearing individuals; but some of them, too, are not
very knowledgeable. This is particularly true of persons who become
dealers so they will have some way of disposing of all the dogs they
accumulated while they were not very knowledgeable collectors.

Which brings us to the point of this book. *The Poor Man's Guide to
Antique Collecting* is designed to help beginning collectors and beginning dealers and those who want to collect but don't have a fortune to
spend, to distinguish between the desirable and the undesirable antiques
(plus a lot of items that are not yet antique but are collectible nevertheless) and to help them identify dozens of newer collectibles that
are appearing or soon will appear in dealers' shops and the for-sale
columns of the collector periodicals.

Most of the things that are described and illustrated in this book are
worth collecting for one reason or another. Some of them are not of
substantial value at this time but may be worth considerably more in
the years ahead. Most of them are plentiful or at least available and
can now be purchased at reasonable prices.

Do not accept the values cited in this book as gospel; use them instead
as a guide. They represent prices recently asked in shops and in the collector periodicals, the reading of whose advertisements is one of my hobbies. Prices asked for the newer collectibles are likely to vary not only
from state to state and city to city, but often from shop to shop within
the same community. Values of traditional antiques from the eighteenth
century on back do not vary nearly so much.

Many of the articles discussed herein may ascend in value somewhat
rapidly within the next few years; some may decline, but with the ranks

of the impecunious collectors swelling at an unprecedented rate, it is not likely that the declines will match the increases. In a number of instances, you will find listed the original selling prices of these trifles and treasures, together with their current estimated values. The former come from the horse's mouth: original advertisements of dealers, wholesalers, and manufacturers in magazines contemporary with their production, or trade catalogues.

There is an old saying that bare walls make giddy housewives, but today bare walls are helping make collectors.

If you're looking for rare Chinese bronzes, Ralph Wood's scarce ceramic figures, or George Ravenscroft's flint glass, you won't find it here. But if nineteenth-century Carlsbad porcelain, Victorian vases, bonbon dishes, pickle casters, and your grandmothers' puff jars interest you, both of us will have a lot of fun in these pages.

Reproductions and Fakes

———————————————⟨◇⟩———————————————

EVERYONE who writes about antiques must have his say on the subject of reproductions and fakes. Happily, I will have less to say about this than most of them. The reason is that the majority of collectible objects that we will discuss in this book have not attained values that make either reproduction or outright faking profitable. So you can see at the outset that if you collect the newer antiques or things that apparently have a good chance of becoming antiques in the not too distant future, there are fewer pitfalls awaiting you than lie in wait for the connoisseur.

Nevertheless, I was appalled a few weeks ago to note on the shelves of gift shops some little footed and plated jewel boxes of that type so popular late last century. Displayed in their pristine newness, they bore price tags of $7.50, or slightly less than the price for which one currently can buy an old one in middling fair condition.

Unmarked reproductions of Carnival glass may send Carnival glass collecting into a tailspin, just as reproductions of certain patterns of pressed glass have frightened many collectors away from these pieces. While some Carnival glass reproductions are identified as such, many others are not.

At the moment, numerous types of art glass first turned out in the last quarter of the nineteenth century are abundant on the market. Most pieces are marked only with paper labels. You would not remove one of these labels with the hope of fooling a gullible buyer and neither would I; but there are—alas!—some individuals who would.

Still, Carnival glass and good art glass bring quite high prices today, so that misrepresentation could be profitable for shady individuals who can collar beginning collectors. I hasten to add that I do not accuse producers of these types of glass with intent to deceive the public. Nevertheless, when they mark their productions only with easily removable paper labels, they are doing no favor to collectors, and I join with many others who have long urged the enactment of legislation that will force manufacturers who reproduce antiques or who reissue their own early wares to mark then indelibly so they will not be mistaken for older pieces.

And don't tell me that there are no dealers who will stoop to simulating signs of age by abrading modern reproductions. I have seen it done. What's more, some reproductions are so good they can occasionally fool even the experts. To make things more confusing, there are many pieces of early glass and other collectible objects around that show no signs of wear, probably because they have been kept carefully in cabinets or tucked safely away elsewhere through the years.

But even if the gift shops are beginning to display reproductions of some of the relatively inexpensive collectible objects originally made in the late nineteenth and early twentieth centuries, it is not very likely that many of these reproductions will be altered by abrading or otherwise and pawned off as originals. And it will not take long for even the inexperienced collector to be able to distinguish between the old and the new by looks and feel. Thus, whereas the pursuer of rare and costly antiques may be forced to employ the services of an expert to help him establish the genuineness of, say, a William and Mary period chair or a Louis Quatorze table, or to make certain there have not been extensive and unheralded alterations, those who seek out the newer collectibles will rarely be put to such expense.

One of the purposes of the present volume is to describe many of the newer collectibles in sufficient detail as to enable them to be spotted and readily identified and to be distinguished from reproductions.

Let me urge you here—and I probably will urge you again later— to handle as many of the objects you intend to collect as possible, so that you will get the "feel" of them, and to read as much as you can about them; for only by constant handling and by obtaining the fullest information possible about antiques or other collectible articles in which you would like to specialize can you yourself become an expert. And if you are to collect profitably, you must become an expert. It's not as difficult as you may think, and I hope this will become more apparent as you read on.

All Is Vanity

THOSE delightful jars, or boxes if you prefer, that you see pictured in this chapter are eye catchers, and the female of the species in particular is likely to be susceptible to them when they are offered for sale in antique shops or shows. They were accouterments of milady's dressing table in years past. You may call them puff jars or puff boxes; in either case you would be correct. The phrases were used interchangeably by manufacturers and dealers. They were designed to hold powder and a puff for its application.

The late nineteenth and early twentieth centuries composed the heyday of the puff jars pictured here, and since they were produced in abundance, they are not particularly scarce. Nevertheless, their values have risen considerably during the past few years and are destined to rise more as the demand for them increases.

These containers not only were produced in a great variety of sizes, shapes, and designs but in a variety of materials—cut glass, pressed glass, pottery, porcelain, and metals, including silver. Thousands of them were made of silver plate.

Particularly desirable are those made of cut glass between 1885 and about 1905—the so-called "Brilliant Period" of American cut glass production—and those of silver. But attractive ones of other materials need not be eschewed. Footed jars in cut glass are more difficult to find today than flat-bottomed ones, but because of the resurgence of demand for

Brilliant cut glass of all kinds, even the latter are becoming rather scarce and prices are rising rapidly.

The cut glass jars were turned out in many of the patterns that have been identified so helpfully in recent years by the late Dorothy Daniel (in her *Cut & Engraved Glass, 1771–1905*) and by other authorities in this field. Most of these had tops of sterling silver, which enhances their appeal and value. Cut glass puff jars were available at the turn of this century at prices ranging roughly from $5.00 to $12.00. Even though their value now is more than double those prices, the same quality jars could not be reproduced today to sell at the prices the original ones are fetching, primarily because of the scarcity and cost of the skilled labor required in their production.

Some of the early cut glass puff boxes had cut glass tops instead of silver ones, but because of the fragility of glass, many of these original tops have been broken and thus lost through the years.

Both the sterling and the silver-plated tops of puff jars in cut and other types of glass and metal were ornately decorated with engraving, embossing, or repoussé. Leaves, flowers, and that frequently recurring bust of the lady with flowing hair that characterized a multitude of creations of the Art Nouveau period are encountered.

Puff jars of crystal glass with sterling tops and gold linings were offered wholesale in 1905 at prices as low as $1.75; today they will bring five times that or more. To find such a jar in satin glass would be a joy, and by no means an impossibility. One of pink satin glass with a sterling silver top was recently offered at $25.00. Satin glass jars of this type appear, however, to be scarce.

Many novel-shaped jars were made of plated silver. Bloomingdale Brothers of New York City offered a round-footed one in its 1892 catalogue at $.98. Those of better quality sold at the turn of this century at wholesale prices of $1.00.

Inexpensive pressed glass boxes with Celluloid tops appeared in quantity in retail shops not long before the outbreak of World War I. From the collector's standpoint, they are not nearly as desirable as the earlier ones. Nor are the cut glass boxes made after about 1915. A great many crystal boxes were made in imitation of earlier cut glass patterns and were sold with silver-plated tops about 1915 for $2.00 or $3.00 each. These will bring $10.00 or more now, a part of the value depending

Early twentieth-century cut glass puff jars with sterling silver and silver-plated tops. These originally cost $4.10 to $6.50 each wholesale, but can still be found today for $10.00 and up.

on how well the silver-plated top has withstood the ravages of time. Some of the tops had small knobs by which they could be lifted.

The average puff box was about three inches tall and measured three or four inches in diameter, although some were larger.

The early pottery and porcelain boxes are scarce. However, you're likely to come across some of these boxes in hand-painted American porcelain made prior to the First World War. Factory hand-painted porcelain was extremely popular in the United States from about 1912 to the 1920s, and the puff boxes, nicely adorned with flowers and sprays, sold at prices of $3.50 to $6.00 and $7.00. They will bring double that or more now if in good condition.

Some boxes also were made with solid silver deposits on them to provide decoration. The silver was deposited electrically on the glass (it could be applied in much the same manner to porcelain and pottery). This so-called silver deposit glass has been of little interest to collectors recently, and a great many pieces may be picked up for a few dollars each. If the silver designs are still in good condition, pieces of this bought judiciously and inexpensively now could prove a neat investment if there is a demand for it in the years ahead as there is likely to be, since scores of our recent ancestors' creations neglected for some years are now moving so rapidly into popularity among the Johnny-come-lately collectors.

There were some high-priced puff jars with lids set with precious or semiprecious stones made last century. These, too, are scarce and you may not find many "sleepers" in this group; but gemstones as investments are mounting in popularity, so keep on the lookout for this type, particularly when you attend a legitimate house sale.

This might be as good a time as any to comment on house sales. Since collecting becomes an addiction for some persons and they buy far more than they have either the physical room or financial resources for, many of these dispose of some of their holdings at sales in their homes to which they invite the public either through newspaper advertisements or handwritten or mimeographed invitations (dispatched primarily to friends and known collectors). Astute collectors will scan the want ad columns of their newspapers regularly for such advertisements and will show up early if not bright at such sales. Frequently you'll encounter bargains in these private homes, but sometimes the items offered are overpriced, either because the zealous collector paid too much herself and doesn't want to take a loss or because she's merely determined to make a profit. At any rate, it's the individual who keeps abreast of values who walks out of such sales with bargains under her arm.

But another type of "house" sale has recently reared its venomous head, and it can be a trap for the unwary. Unscrupulous dealers will rent a house in a residential section, stock it with antiques or other items, few indeed of which are bargains, and will then advertise a "private house sale." Sometimes the dealers will employ a sweet little old lady to sell the items for them, inducing her to represent herself as the owner.

The precaution that should be taken to keep yourself from falling into such a trap is to maintain a list of the addresses at which such sales are advertised in your community over a period of time. When you see the same address listed time after time, you can be reasonably certain that this is no periodic house sale but represents the machinations of a fellow out for the kill. And, human nature being what it is, you'll occasionally find individuals selling from their own homes regularly, advertising their sales as "house sales" and thereby escaping the purchase of a dealer's license and the payment of taxes. Shady characters enter even the nicest businesses.

And as long as we got up on the wrong side of the bed this morning, we might as well point out, also, that you may encounter some antique auction sales that are not entirely aboveboard. Some operators employ shills in the audience to bid prices up. Such auctioneers are often able to knock down items to exuberant bidders whose enthusiasm has been fired red hot by the competitive bids of the hired hand, at excessive prices. Naturally this practice is frowned on by the well-known and established auctioneers, but it exists nevertheless.

You'll find some auctioneers, too, who will refuse to accept starting bids on expensive pieces that do not at least equal what the auctioneer or his company paid for them. It is a fact, of course, that a great many auctioneers sell both their own merchandise and that which has been consigned to them for sale by others. The conscientious auctioneer will try to get the best price he can for whatever he sells, regardless of who owns it; but the reputable auctioneer will not employ shady devices to send bids soaring. So watch yourself, and watch the audience too.

Now that we have that out of our system, let's proceed to another member of the same family to which the puff jar belongs—the hair receiver.

Hair receivers were widely utilized in the days before the advent of bobbed and short hair to receive the strands that clung to the comb or brush when milady made her toilet. Many, but not all, hair receivers were fitted with a lid with a hole in its center through which the

Silver-plated hair receiver as advertised in 1900. This one was gold-lined with a removable top.

strands could be dropped into the receptacle beneath. These little containers were made of the same materials as were the puff jars. Some were footed, and many of the glass receivers had sterling silver or silver-plated lids or tops. Although most were round, some were oblong or square.

A number of hair receivers also were produced in hand-painted porcelain. Some were made by a company operated by Reinhold Schlegemilch in Germany and are marked "RS Prussia" with a red star. (Later ones of this type are marked "RS Germany," and the same productions also are marked with the name "Tillowitz.") The Schlegemilch factory was located in Tillowitz in Silesia, now a part of Poland.

The RS Prussia pieces are beautifully hand-painted, often with floral motifs, and the porcelain is of good quality. Some pieces bear the marks of their decorators, usually their initials. Some whiteware pieces were decorated in this country. The ware has a soft glaze and is quite attractive. In recent years it has caught the fancy of collectors, and prices have spiraled upward. You are likely to have to pay $20.00 to $35.00 for a hair receiver. The pieces marked RS Germany are often lower in price, but the value of these, too, is now upward. Sometimes you'll find pieces with the name Tillowitz which also bear the mark "Silesia," or with other markings. Large quantities of these wares were imported years ago into the United States, but the clamor for them in the last few years has been so great that they are now becoming somewhat elusive.

The C. F. Monroe Company of Meriden, Connecticut, made both hair receivers and puff boxes in its now well-known Wave Crest ware—painted opal glassware made from opaque white glass. The glass was blown into full-size molds and decorated. These also will bring good prices—ten to fifteen times the $4.80 for which the puff jars wholesaled in 1907. One type of puff box made in Wave Crest ware contained a mirror that could be utilized when the top was raised. Because of high current prices, it is somewhat depressing to thumb back through the pages of *The Youth's Companion* for 1901 to find a Wave Crest puff jar offered for $.85.

Early in this century many inexpensive porcelain toilet sets were produced with several pieces in matching patterns. These customarily consisted of a dresser tray, a puff box (and sometimes a hair receiver), cologne bottle, ring stand, and smaller pin tray. Hundreds of such sets retailed for less than $2.00 originally. You'll be fortunate to find one for less than about fifteen or twenty times that amount today.

There are still available, however, numerous silver-plated, pressed glass, and porcelain puff jars and hair receivers at prices ranging from around $7.50 to $20.00.

Puff jars and hair receivers make attractive and interesting accessories for the dressing table, and one can place them into service today as containers for jewelry, buttons, pins, sewing adjuncts, and a host of other small objects that the lady of the house likes to have easily accessible.

Although you'll have to shell out more cash for the sterling silver, cut glass, and art glass types than for types that were originally less expensive, you may find them better investments.

The higher-priced pieces will be found in scores of antique shops, but your best bet for the more commonplace puff jars and hair receivers is the newly opened shop whose proprietor has limited capital and prefers to offer a large number of relatively inexpensive items rather than a few high-priced ones. These pieces also are frequently among household effects found at auction sales in the smaller cities and are often found at the house sales we mentioned earlier. Better still, ask one of your elderly aunts if she doesn't have a puff jar or a hair receiver stored away among her effects of yesteryear. Chances are she may, unless she's much younger than she looks.

Hand and Foot

I DON'T know why the delightful glove buttoner—almost a necessity when "dressing up" in years past—has been thus far so largely neglected; but it is indeed a collectible object.

Buttonhooks have been collected for some years, but the glove buttoner, which it so closely resembles, still awaits large-scale collecting. The same holds true for the late nineteenth- and early twentieth-century shoehorn, which helped many a man and many a maid fit oversized feet into undersized shoes.

A collector named Bertha L. Betensley, of Chicago, has written an interesting booklet about buttonhooks. It is entitled *Buttonhooks to Trade—to Treasure,* and it is filled with information about these adjuncts of high-button shoes; but as far as I know, no one has yet seen fit to write a book about shoehorns or exclusively about glove buttoners. This is too bad, and I hope this chapter will help overcome that deficiency.

One nice thing about collecting glove buttoners and shoehorns is that you can display dozens of them in a fairly small space. Unlike iron kettles, large paintings, and copper boilers, they do not sprawl about your premises and take over your home or cause the floors to sag.

Early glove buttoners looked more or less like a piece of looped wire with a twisted handle, which is just about what they were. The loop was large at the top and tapered at the bottom. A bit later, glove buttoners (you may call them glove hooks if you wish) took on the same shape as buttonhooks used to fasten button shoes. The primary difference was that the former was smaller. This type had a handle, a shaft, and a curved hook on the end. They were even used interchangeably.

Glove buttoners—the loop type—were made in the late nineteenth century with chains, to one end of which the fastener loop was attached.

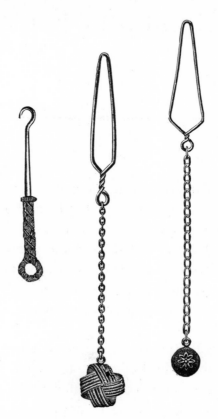

Glove buttoners. These were loops of wire, often with chains and charms attached. Glove hooks, smaller versions of the buttonhook, came a few years later. They usually had handles of ornamented sterling or silver plate.

To the other end was attached a charm. These could be worn on milady's shirtwaist or coat. Some charms were set with various types of stones and looked quite elegant.

The buttoners featured handles made out of various materials—silver, silver plate, wood, horn, ivory, gold, and plastics. Plastics are not as young as you think: commercial plastics were developed in America more than a century ago. The handles also came in some fantastic designs. Many silver and silver-plated ones were lavishly decorated by engraving or embossing, and some were further embellished with imitation stones, the imitation amethyst being a favorite.

Some buttoners were made as combination pieces in conjunction with small knives and could be folded into a compact case. Some were attached to and worn with bracelets. Some featured tassels on the end.

In earlier days the man of the house was not averse to borrowing his wife's glove buttoner to help him button his stiff white shirt, probably washed and ironed by the same laundry that invariably puts too much starch in my own shirts.

Small gold-plated buttoners with silk tassels attached sold in 1890 for as little as half a dollar. In the same year, you could have bought rolled gold buttoners with intriguing charms attached at prices of about $1.75 to $3.50. Those with fine sterling handles were wholesaling at prices of from $2.00 to $3.00.

Some fancy glove buttoners were sold last century in plush-lined cases. Others were made a part of manicure sets, although the connection between buttoning one's gloves and manicuring one's nails is a trifle vague.

Shoehorns have been turned out through the years by the hundreds of thousands and are far more plentiful than glove buttoners; yet some of them were fancy affairs indeed and should not be sneezed at by the collector, incipient or experienced. The eclectic collector is bound to be puzzled by the fact that so many of his predecessors have collected buttonhooks but have ignored shoehorns. Perhaps the reason is that nobody had told them before about shoehorns as I am telling you now. I think shoehorns are coming in as collectors' items, especially the ornate ones and those with handles in the Art Nouveau style, which currently seems to be attracting its share of collectors.

There are thousands of plain, simple nickel and other metal shoehorns that were once given free to customers by shoe stores and other establishments as gestures of good will, and many persons would never have got their shoes on without them. A lot of these bear advertising for the emporia that gave them away. Since interesting examples of early American advertising art are now being eagerly sought by both individuals and institutions, this type is bound to ascend in value pretty soon. But right now you can pick up many of them for a pittance; some have been offered for a dollar or less. A large collection of differ-

Shoehorns made at the turn of the century. Those at the top have sterling silver handles and nickel-plated steel blades. The horn and hook set at bottom right has ebony handles with silver mounts.

ent advertising shoehorns would be something to talk about and to show to the minister when he came to Sunday dinner.

Of more monetary value, of course, would be a collection of horns with sterling silver handles. At the turn of this century you could buy these for a dollar or two; but of late silver has gone up, up, up.

Those with decorated silver-plated handles are much easier to find and cost less. Shoehorns also were turned out with handles of ivory, pearl, bone, and other materials. These are desirable—and scarcer. And don't ignore those with early plastic handles.

You are not likely to find a great many glove buttoners or shoehorns in antique shops at this time, but there are probably many of them stashed away in old homes. Try your older relatives first; then pick on your older friends.

Chances are you can buy desirable glove buttoners currently at prices ranging upward from about $2.00, with the more elaborate ones and those with handles of amber, glass, and sterling coming higher. Certain types of shoehorns now going at a dollar or so will increase a good bit in value before long if enough persons take to heart what I have just written about them.

Sweets for the Sweet

WE hardly dare talk about the agreeableness of sweets today in other than muted tones. No matter how pleasurable to our palate may be the bonbon, the sugarplum, and the cherry tart swimming in a sea of seductive whipped cream, when we reach for one we are warned of the dangers of coronary thrombosis, hypertension, ventricular hypertrophy, and other assorted diseases as difficult to pronounce as they are to spell. So we eschew the delectable tidbit and remain, as best we can, pallid, thin, and ravenous.

It was not always so. Buxomness was once admired in the female and the pleasingly plump male was rarely frowned upon so long as he did not reach butterball proportions.

The laden tables of our ancestors frequently were graced with confection dishes (also called bonbon dishes and/or trays), especially when there was company for dinner. These have been succeeded today by vitamin pill bottles and Metrecal cans, and one day perhaps these bottles and cans may become collectible, but it will certainly be in the distant future. But the confection dish is collectible right now, although it seems to have been largely overlooked in the midst of the rush to acquire salt and pepper shakers, pattern tumblers, spoon holders, and patent medicine bottles.

Confection or bonbon dishes were made of glass, including cut glass, silver and plated silver, and porcelain and earthenware, and in almost every shape one can imagine. The word "dish" is a catchall; these

Bonbon dishes and boxes. Three 1892 boxes on top row. The one on extreme right was of sterling, gold-lined, and costly—$11.00 wholesale. The silver-plated one on the extreme left wholesaled for $.35. Second row, from left: silver-plated box with embossed flower; "Whist" pattern in cut glass; and "Corinthian" pattern in cut glass. Third row: silver-plated and gold-lined basket; silver-plated jar with removable cover; and handled silver-plated basket. Bottom row: handled jar; handled silver-plated basket; and footed silver-plated dish. All date in the 1890s except the ones of cut glass, which were offered in 1914.

containers took the form of bowls, baskets, trays, and boxes. In addition to the larger containers used on the table to hold sweets, there were tiny bonbon boxes that could be carried in one's purse. These often were used to hold such things as mints to sweeten one's breath and were akin to the English comfit boxes used to hold sweetmeats and bonbons.

The heyday of the bonbon dish and box in the United States was the late nineteenth century, although they were carried over in some numbers into the first quarter of the present one.

Bonbon boxes for the purse were most often of silver and had hinged and lavishly decorated tops. Most of them measured less than two inches in diameter and less than half an inch in height. Some of these in sterling silver were available in the 1890s at about $5.00 each, but plated ones could be purchased for well under a dollar. The latter today are worth several dollars each in good condition and those of sterling, a good bit more, but they are hard to find.

Much more abundant are the confection containers designed for table use. Naturally their use was not confined to the dinner table; they once found their place in the living room and the parlor so that members of the family or their guests might appease their sweet tooth after eating more mundane foods.

In 1914, an attractive heart-shaped dish of cut glass appeared in a pattern called Whist. It measured five inches in diameter and was advertised as a "bonbon or olive" dish. Its wholesale price was $1.80. There was being marketed at about the same time a handled cut glass "bonbon or butter ball" dish in the Corinthian pattern. It came in two sizes—six- and seven-inch diameters—and these wholesaled at $7.50 and $9.75, respectively.

Silver-plated bonbon containers abounded between 1885 and 1910. Scores of smaller ones were quite inexpensive, bearing wholesale price tags of from about $1.75 to $3.00. Larger and more elaborate dishes wholesaled from $5.00 to $7.00. A choice confection compote on a tall standard (eight and a half inches high) was offered in 1905 at a wholesale price of $5.00.

Quite a number of these silver-plated containers were gold-lined and decorated by embossing. Some came with bail-type handles (loops), and some with small feet. The illustrations will afford an idea of the diversity of shapes and designs in which they were produced. Those containing the heaviest deposit of silver over their base metal were termed "quadruple plate." Those with a somewhat thinner silver deposit were referred to as "triple plate."

It is not at all unlikely that you may encounter some of the silver-plated dishes whose coat of silver has tarnished and worn thin, at prices not in excess of and perhaps even lower than those for which they originally retailed. But collectors now are discovering that articles with badly worn silver plate can be replated and made handsome accessories for the home.

Some shops recently have had silver-plated bonbon trays available priced at just $5.00 or $6.00, although those whose silver coat is in good condition will bring more.

Since the price of fine cut glass continues to go up, it may pay you to look carefully for such dishes at home sales, auctions, and the antique shops. Occasionally, though not often, you may find a sleeper at a flea market. But as more persons enter this field of collecting and become knowledgeable about their specialties, the chances of finding sleepers diminish considerably. Don't be too greedy; take a chance occasionally, just as you do when you buy stocks or make other investments.

You can use the purse-size bonbon boxes for toting around small pins or even bonbons that you can devour on the sly. If this hurts your conscience, carry your vitamin pills in them. The larger ones can be used to hold fruit and various other edibles. These can also be used as card receivers if you still observe this amenity.

The C. F. Monroe Company, mentioned in a preceding chapter, also made a Wave Crest handled bonbon dish. This originally wholesaled for $3.00, but you will be lucky if you find one today for less than about $50.00, and by the time you read this, the price may be more.

One of the best places in which to find silver-plated dishes and trays of various kinds is the establishment specializing in secondhand merchandise. The reason is that many owners of worn silver-plated objects look upon them as of no value, because collectors have thus far largely side-stepped them. It will not always be thus.

Special bonbon spoons and tongs should also be watched for and can be collected right along with the boxes and dishes.

A group of silver-plated bonbon containers, all dating around the turn of the century. The compote is quite desirable.

Here's a word of advice: when you shop around in secondhand stores and at the retail establishments operated by such institutions as the Goodwill Industries, look carefully at the metal pieces you may find heavily coated with dust. You'll sometimes find a little treasure beneath the grime that has accumulated with the years. Small secondhand stores with only one or two employees simply don't have the time or manpower to examine with great care and clean and shine up all the miscellaneous items they buy from homes. If they did, they'd probably up considerably the prices of those that suddenly assumed a delightful appearance when the dust, grease, and paint had been removed.

Silver-plated confection dishes that look hopelessly worn and dismal will often brighten under your tender ministrations with the aid of luke-warm water. But should you find that the silver plate has worn through in many spots, you'd better either ignore the piece or reconcile yourself to the fact that you'll have to have it replated, which can sometimes cost you more than you pay for a piece. Nevertheless, if the plated piece is handsome enough and old enough, replating can add substantially to its value, purists to the contrary.

You may be surprised at how many times you find a plated confection dish well coated with grime for one or two dollars that can be converted by polishing or replating into an object worth $25 or more. Rummaging the secondhand stores is not a sport for those who are squeamish about dirtying their hands; and if you pursue the establishments on the run-down side streets, leave your best bib and tucker at home and don something that is easily washable. The treasures you may thus accumulate will pay your laundry bill many times over.

Nutty but Nice

———————⟨◇⟩———————

THERE are several specialized types of dishes akin to bonbon containers awaiting the collector's eager grasp. Since most of these were popular at about the same time, and since some of them were used interchangeably despite their individual appellations, let's consider the group together in this chapter.

The category includes nut stands, orange dishes, fruit and berry bowls, and jelly dishes. You could lump several of these together and simply call them fancy dishes. Some manufacturers did.

Berry bowls of decorated glass, cut glass, and art glass in fancy metal holders were turned out by the carload late last century and through the first decade or so of this one, and thousands of these were and are utterly delightful. These bowls stood on the dining tables of probably the majority of middle- and upper-class homes during those years in which they were produced in such profusion. Manufacturers called them either berry bowls or fruit bowls; and some termed them "berry or fruit" bowls. Collectors today call a lot of these bowls "bride's baskets," since they proved popular as wedding gifts in years past.

These bowls and their silver-plated stands were truly ornamental pieces, and because many of them featured bowls of colored, shaded, and decorated glass, they imparted color to a room. The majority of the bowls had pleated or ruffled edges. In the latter part of the nineteenth century, they largely replaced the more cumbersome (but never-

Fruit or berry dishes of the 1890s. The one at top left has a bowl of fancy decorated colored glass and the one at right is opaque white glass. Just above them in the center is a cut glass berry bowl. The bowls in the second row are of crystal and opaque white glass. The bowls in the bottom row, from left: crystal glass, imported pink glass, and decorated ruby glass. The silver-plated stands in the bottom row were manufactured by William A. Rogers and the others by Homan Silver Plate Company.

theless fascinating) epergnes as dining table centerpieces. They could be utilized singly or in pairs.

Bowls were made of satin glass, cranberry glass, various types of shaded glass, clear crystal (usually decorated by enameling or other means), crackle glass, and other types. Some bowls of overlay glass boasted one color on the inside and another on the outside.

Favorite colors included rose, greens, amethyst, blue, ruby, and ivory. The bowls came in various sizes, ranging from as small as about four inches in diameter to twelve inches or more.

The bowls were made by glasshouses in the United States and abroad, large numbers having been imported from Europe. The stands were manufactured by numerous silver-plate makers of the nineteenth century and were usually ornately decorated, their handles in particular having been designed in imaginative shapes. Bases were sometimes round or oval, sometimes square or oblong, and not infrequently footed.

Some of these charming bowl-stand sets wholesaled at the turn of this century for as little as $2.50, and dozens were available in a price range, wholesale, of from $4.80 to $7.90. Today, they are worth $40.00 to about $100.00 on the collectors' market, depending upon their size, the type of glass, and their condition. One problem is that the bowls and the stands became separated often during the years, with the result that you may often encounter bowls today without stands and stands without bowls; but it can be fun buying a bowl and then shopping around for a stand that fits and matches. Bowls alone can sometimes be found in out-of-the-way shops for under $25.00, but many others are worth $35.00 up.

We bought our latest (and I suspect our last) berry bowl and stand at an auction in 1968. I say "last," because there was a little problem. My wife saw the bowl before the sale started and intended to bid on it. Omniscient in such matters, I advised her the top price to bid was $45.00, because if we should decide to sell it, we couldn't get more than that for it. Unfortunately, just as the bowl and stand were put up for sale, in walked a gentleman who at several preceding sales had bid successfully against us for a lot of glass wares we wanted. Consequently, he was not in our good graces, to put it mildly.

Thereupon, my good woman (who will undoubtedly thrash me when she sees this in print) informed me that she intended to have the bowl

Some of these jelly dishes look almost exactly like fruit and berry bowls; the principal difference is size. Those in the top two rows were made in 1907, the two at the left on the bottom, in 1891, and the one at the right, in 1890. The jelly server is sterling (1907).

Two jelly knives of sterling (1907), a sterling jelly spoon (1900), and a New Century berry spoon (1900), with a 1907 York pattern silver-plated jelly shell below.

and stand regardless of the price they fetched, because she was tired of being outbid. She did get the set—at $65.00, which was then and probably still is $20.00 more than it is worth. This is a major reason for not letting your emotions get the better of you at auction sales.

The bowls and stands can serve a variety of purposes in today's home, including that for which they were originally intended. Or they can be used advantageously to hold floral arrangements or merely to grace the room.

Since the demand for good art glass is now at a peak, an investment in some of these bowls could be well worth while.

Nut bowls and jelly dishes were made both of glass and of silver, or, in greater numbers, plated silver. Some of the jelly dishes are exactly like the fruit and berry bowls except that they are smaller. Many nut dishes were decorated with the image of a squirrel, usually eating nuts, along the rim or at a handle. A collection of squirrel-adorned nut bowls could be fascinating. Some were produced in crystal glass imitating cut glass patterns. Orange stands or dishes were very like the nut stands.

A few berry bowls and stands came complete with a special berry spoon, and so did some jelly dishes; but individual berry and jelly spoons and servers were manufactured by silversmiths and silver-plating firms in great abundance.

There are many souvenir spoon collectors, but I find certain other types of spoons—including some berry and jelly spoons—just as intriguing, and I think you also may. Some of them are pictured here for your delectation.

Of course, berry and jelly bowls also were made in cut glass and are currently selling at fairly high prices, certainly as compared to what they were bringing ten years ago.

I hope some of the bowls and dishes pictured in this chapter will make your mouth water. Mine started drooling after I finished the first paragraph, and I already have some of the bowls. But I'd like to have a lot more. By and large, the silver-plated dishes of the types about which we have been writing here are available at prices considerably less than those of glass; some with worn silver should be available for a very few dollars.

Peter Piper Picked a Peck

AN interesting dining adjunct of our grandparents was the caster (also spelled "castor" and often referred to as a condiment container or, when more than one was used, as a condiment set).

A caster is a cruet or vial or an allied container designed to hold condiments. Casters were (and still are) used for oil and vinegar, salt, pepper, and such.

Casters were produced in sets of several bottles or vials and also individually. Sets contained from two to five vials or, more rarely, six. Smaller sets were sometimes called breakfast casters and larger sets were often referred to as dinner casters. The sets were housed in silver or silver-plated frames with a base and handle.

Caster sets have been collected for some time, and our concern here will not be primarily with the large set or the salt-and-pepper caster but rather with a perfectly fascinating type called the pickle caster, because it was designed to hold the very things that Peter Piper picked a peck of.

Pickle caster sets were made with either one or two glass containers, most frequently round, and included a pair of tongs which eliminated the necessity of grasping the pickles in the fingers; this was not particularly sanitary anyway. Thousands of utterly intriguing pickle casters were turned out late last century and through the first quarter of this one by United States silver-plating companies, which usually made the frames and purchased the glass containers from glasshouses.

1907 pickle casters in silver-plated frames. The two on each end are by Homan Silver Plate Company and the two in the center by E. G. Webster & Sons.

A large percentage of the glass jars were made of colored and decorated glass, ruby, or cranberry, having been a favorite. Many were charmingly decorated with enamels. Floral designs predominated but were not exclusively used.

The frames undoubtedly taxed many a designer's imagination, and most of those made in the nineteenth century reflected the interest in the rococo that prevailed at that time. In addition to the silver or plated bases and frames, the containers themselves were provided with decorated tops or lids, which almost always had a finial by which they could be lifted. Some frames and lids were also made of Britannia metal or late pewter. Britannia metal is a white alloy of tin, copper, and antimony, with a little zinc customarily added. It resembles in appearance pewter, to which it is closely akin, but is produced by spinning, whereas pewter is produced by casting. Although the majority of containers were of glass, some also were made of porcelain.

The use of casters actually dates back to the eighteenth century, but the collector without a fortune to share with the dealer will have to be content with those made from the last half of the last century. And almost any collector should be content with choice examples of those.

In addition to enameled and otherwise decorated colored glass, you may stumble across pickle casters of Pearl Satin glass if you have been attending church regularly.

About the beginning of the twentieth century, you could buy choice pickle casters for $4.00 to $10.00. Choice pickle casters with frames in good condition will now set you back $25.00 to $75.00 or so, depending upon the quality of the frame and of the glass. Occasionally you'll come across advertisements in the collector periodicals listing pickle casters at less than $25.00 and you may find a few in shops at less than that figure, but the price trend is upward. Certainly you won't find one with a jar of Pearl Satin glass for such a low price and you'll have difficulty in locating any in pattern glass for a pittance. Still, do what the experts do: pay a fast visit to all those new shops that keep opening with such remarkable optimism. You may find a dealer specializing in primitives who has a pickle caster on hand and isn't aware of its value. Today, however, this is a mighty big maybe, but the possibility still exists. One morning I visited a shop that featured primarily such stuff as iron kettles, churns, and stoneware jugs and picked up a Wedgwood Jasperware medallion for $7.50. The dealer said she had no idea what it was. This could pose a question of ethics. Should you enlighten the dealer or should you buy it and keep your mouth shut. I did a little of both. I said:

"It's a mighty pretty piece and I guess it's worth more than you're asking, so I'll take it."

Multi-bottle caster sets are often found minus one or two of the original bottles, which leaves you with the necessity of hunting around for matching bottles. This could take a year or more. Most pickle casters are found with original frame and jar intact, since at the outset there were two bottles at most to lose or break, and in most cases only one. Besides, these sets were so attractive that their owners took good care of them and probably kept them off the tables when small children were around. I would advise you to do the same.

Our illustrations provide you with only a small sampling of the wondrous variety in which these pickle casters were produced. Don't forget that if the frame of a set you find has badly worn spots, you can have it replated. I don't care what the purists say about this: a fine pickle jar in a replated frame looks much better than one in a frame that looks as if the cat had dragged it through the barnyard.

Pickle casters are not yet extremely scarce, because so many of them were made, but good ones are becoming increasingly difficult to find, and if you want to sink some of your surplus funds in them, I think you'll find them a good investment from the standpoints of both pleasure and monetary profit in the years ahead.

As for the larger caster sets, if you are a fairly patient individual, you can make the best buy by dickering with dealers for sets that lack one or two bottles or that contain a cracked bottle. With a little luck and a lot of perseverance, you are likely, sooner or later, to find the matching bottles you need. Sets with bottles that lack stoppers also can be bought more cheaply than those with their stoppers intact. Small antiques shops often have miscellaneous glass stoppers, along with stocks of miscellaneous hardware, so that one day you are likely to encounter the very stopper you need.

Time on Your Hands

I WILL not attempt to explain this phenomenon, but there is currently a run on wooden-case kitchen clocks—those gingerbread ugly ducklings that flourished in the 1880s and took on their worst appearance about 1910. Don't rush out and buy these affairs because I told you to, since I am not telling you to at all; but apparently I am one of the few persons in the country who is not telling you to.

They really weren't kitchen clocks. They were called wood mantel clocks, and they once sat in many a living room, but I cannot possibly see how they graced it. However, I am not going to fight the tide of public opinion, and you can acquire one or a dozen of these clocks if you wish.

I call them kitchen clocks because I wouldn't put one in any other room of my home and I am not sure I would put it in the kitchen.

These clocks had scrolled wooden cases and inexpensive works and most of them operated about eight days on a full winding. Most of the cases were of either oak or walnut. Some struck on the hour and others struck each half hour, provided you kept the striking mechanism wound.

Thousands of these clocks wholesaled in 1900 for less than $5.00 each; others had wholesale prices of $5.00 to $6.00. The Waterbury Clock Company made a line of them that wholesaled as this century opened for only $19.00 for a case of six. Ten or fifteen years ago you couldn't give these clocks away, but right now they are selling for

$35.00 to $65.00; and in my neck of the woods I doubt that one of them has sold at auction for less than about $30.00 in the past year. I would not be at all surprised if by the time you read this, some of these clocks were selling at $75.00 or more.

Nearly all the big clock companies produced them, including, in addition to Waterbury, the Seth Thomas, New Haven, Gilbert, Sessions, and Ansonia clock companies.

Although they all looked pretty much alike from a distance, there were variations in their glued-on wooden decorations and the decoration of the cases.

The clocks featured a pendulum, which could be viewed through a glass front on the case provided the glass was not too heavily decorated. Gilt decorations took the form of flowers and vines, Gothic arches, urns of classic shapes, geometrical designs, and even pelicans and bulrushes.

Some of the so-called "better" clocks of this type had calendar dials, so that you could not only tell the time but the date by them. Others had inexpensive thermometers attached to one side of the case in front and still others had a thermometer on one side and a spirit level on the other. Frequently, clocks with chimes cost $.50 extra. A lot of these clocks were equipped with alarms, which, in some cases, added another $.50 to the cost. Most of the bells were of wire.

Various makes of these clocks bore some fascinating names, among them, Buffalo, Gibson, Level, Tampa, Niles, Jamaica, Sampson, Medea, Oxford, Yale, Harvard, Cambridge, Fruit, and Geranium. Many were named after cities—New York, Urbana, Utica, Concord, Oakland, and so on. Some were named after politicians, statesmen, and Presidents, including Washington, Lincoln, Polk, Grant, and Clay. There also were Great Lakes sets—Erie, Ontario, Michigan, Huron, and Superior. Personally, I prefer the Jarvis, because it sounds like something no clock should ever have been named.

In spite of their looks, these clocks were good timekeepers, and their mechanisms were so simple they rarely got out of order. You can pick them up now at auctions and shops in fine running condition after sixty or seventy years.

Perhaps the fact that they still run appeals to many individuals. Possibly others buy them because they impart a rustic look to the living room mantel. At any rate, they have been selling like hot cakes with

Gilbert Clock Company's eight-day wood mantel clocks of 1900. These "beauties" were distinguished by scrollwork and wooden decoration glued to the frame.

prices creeping up but still within a range that does not put too big a bite on the bank account.

Probably the worst geographical section of the country in which to look for these clocks is the South. The reason is not that they will not be found there but that inexpensive clocks in general bring higher prices in Dixie than they do in New England, Pennsylvania, and points north.

Try the shops in the smaller New England communities, and also try the shops of clock repairmen, who often buy up this type, put them in operating order, and sell them for less than the going price in antiques shops.

If you decide to bid on these clocks at auction in the South, fix yourself a maximum bid limit before the sale begins. Otherwise, you may find that the spirited bidding of those who simply cannot resist the wood mantel clock will send the prices up beyond reason.

In conscience, I cannot advise you to buy such clocks as ornaments for your home, but unless the current trend abruptly reverses itself, you may be able to make a few bucks by selling those you may be able to buy for $20.00 or $25.00 in New England to an eager Southerner for $50.00 or $60.00. This is not a fortune, but it is not a bad profit either. You can advertise them for sale in one of the collector periodicals for a very small fee. If you do, remember to point out that the cost of shipping is to be paid by the purchaser.

Unless you are an expert tinkerer, I'd advise you not to buy clocks with any missing parts. You may or may not be able to find the parts you need; and if you can't, you're simply stuck with an out-of-order clock.

File—but Don't Forget

COLLECTORS have been so busy pursuing the traditional antiques that they have overlooked such apparently prosaic objects as the nail file and the nail buff. Yet these plebeian articles took on an aura of glamor under the ministrations of late nineteenth-century designers and workmen, and we commend them to you for a long, hard look.

There are, in fact, other adjuncts of the manicure set of less than a century ago that deserve the collector's scrutiny, among them the humble corn knife and the helpful cuticle blade, both of which, encased in a silver or silver-plated handle, assumed a respectability that gained them entrance to the better boudoirs.

Yet we shall content ourselves here with the file and the buff, not, of course, with the expectation that you will toss out your collection of Carnival glass and gold snuffboxes but with the hope that you may find here a new field of interest that you may be among the first to cultivate.

Particularly interesting are nail files with sterling silver handles and skin buffs with sterling mounts, but there is no need to pass by those of plated silver either, or even those with handles of pearl.

Anticipating mass production techniques, manufacturers of silver and silver-plated objects late last century began designing elaborate "stock" handles into which could be fitted steel nail files, cuticle knives, nail brushes, buttonhooks, and even toothbrushes. These were turned out in a tremendous variety of shapes, designs, and sizes, and were

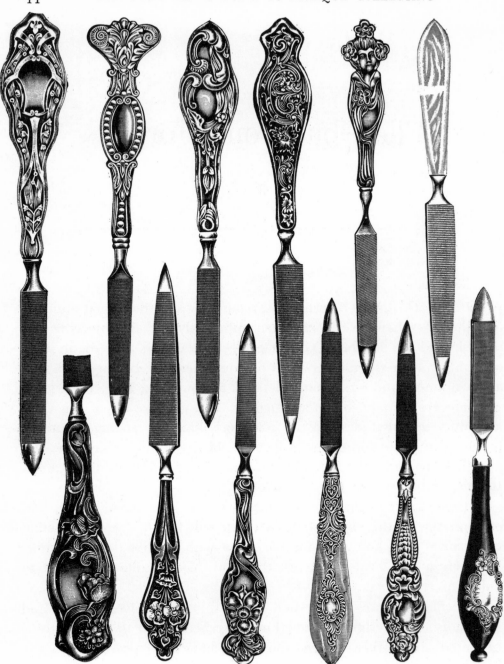

These nail files were made between 1899 and 1908. All have sterling silver handles except the one at top right (pearl) and that at bottom right (ebony). The handle at the extreme left, bottom row, was designed to hold interchangeable accessories.

embossed with the flowers, vines, and geometrical-type figures so be-loved of that period. Some were also graced with female heads fashioned almost like a finial or the handle of a souvenir spoon. Actually, these files should hold the same fascination for collectors as do souvenir spoons, and you should be able to pick up some silver-plated ones for a dollar or two if you begin seeking them now before the rush sets in.

Early in the present century, steel files with sterling silver or white pearl handles were offered dealers at wholesale prices of $5.00 to $12.00 a dozen, depending upon size and the "elegance" of the work-manship. By about 1909, wholesale prices of those with sterling handles had risen to as much as $15.00 a dozen and those with fine pearl handles, to $2.00 each. In 1900, dealers could buy sterling-handled cuticle knives for as little as $.21.

Probably less desirable from the viewpoint of the collector, but pos-sessed of some merit nevertheless, were files with ebonized wooden handles decorated with sterling silver shields or mounts. In 1900, these wholesaled for a dollar. And, of course, there were small steel nail files that folded into sterling or silver-plated cases. These wholesaled for $7.00 to $12.00 a dozen as the century began.

Chamois skin buffs in the 1890s and early 1900s were fitted with sterling or plated handles and ranged in length from around three to five and a half inches. The late Art Nouveau style was reflected early in this century in the sinuous vines and attenuated flowers that served as their decoration. Handles were fashioned in a diversity of shapes, which will lend great interest to a collection of the buffs.

The wholesale price range in 1900 for attractive sterling buffs was about $1.35 to $3.00, although there were some with handles made of a material called "silveroin" that imitated sterling, that wholesaled for $.84 each, and there were even less expensive ones with black ebony handles with silver shields. One of these is listed in a 1900 catalogue at $.68.

In addition to being sold individually, files and buffs often were included as a part of packaged manicure sets that also contained such other accessories as scissors, corn knives, buttonhooks, shoehorns, and sometimes toothbrushes, pomade jars, puff boxes, and hair curlers. Benj. Allen & Company of Chicago offered an elaborate manicure set of fourteen pieces in a cloth-lined leatherette case in 1905 for a wholesale price of $32.00, but less sumptuous sets were available at $5.00 or so.

Our illustrations will tell you much more about the files and buffs than we can with words. Although you are likely to find few of these manicure accessories in antiques shops, you should be able to stumble across them in many older homes or among the possessions of older families, including the elderly relatives in your own. You may also find them in secondhand establishments and junk shops, whose owners have kept them around just because they hate to throw anything away.

Look for manicure sets or parts of sets in well-worn cases that present an unattractive appearance and, because of this, are probably priced very low. After all, you want the contents, not the case. You'll probably find extremely low price tags on nail buffs whose chamois skin has been well worn; but remember that you want the handles, not the chamois.

In addition, the word about the coming vogue for Art Nouveau has probably not yet filtered down to all the small antiques dealers in fairly isolated communities, so that they may not be nearly as intrigued by those decorations of sinuous vines and languid ladies with flowing hair as you or your neighbor or the lady in the next block who reads the collector magazines assiduously and knows what styles are enjoying a revival.

These manicure accessories are things to hold onto for a while until someone writes a book about them. Then watch the prices rise as a lot of hands reach out for them.

The Horsey Set

IT has been some time since the village smithy stood under a spreading chestnut tree and flexed muscles that were as tough as iron bands, if indeed he ever did, Longfellow notwithstanding.

Faithful Dobbin, to whose iron shoes the smith attended with an eagerness bred of the necessity of earning a livelihood, has not yet disappeared from the American scene, but he is well on his way out along with his sister Maud.

Blacksmiths in the tail half of the twentieth century are indeed a vanishing breed too, and somehow it seems a pity. The only blacksmith I have seen recently has been on television, but there are undoubtedly others around the country.

The blacksmith contributed much to the progress of America, for, although the youngsters reared on a diet of sports cars may not know it, his work had to do with much more than horses. Our early blacksmith wrought objects ranging from fireplace utensils to plows, and without his skill as a repairman, many a metal home necessity would have gone into the discard pile before it had paid its way.

Undoubtedly, many of the fire tongs, fireplace cranes and trammels, skillets, and other metal adjuncts of living and doing of much earlier days that we now encounter in museums and antiques shops specializing in primitives were fashioned by the skillful hands of blacksmiths.

I have not been fond of horses since one ran away with the milk wagon in which I was sitting in Greensboro, North Carolina. But I do

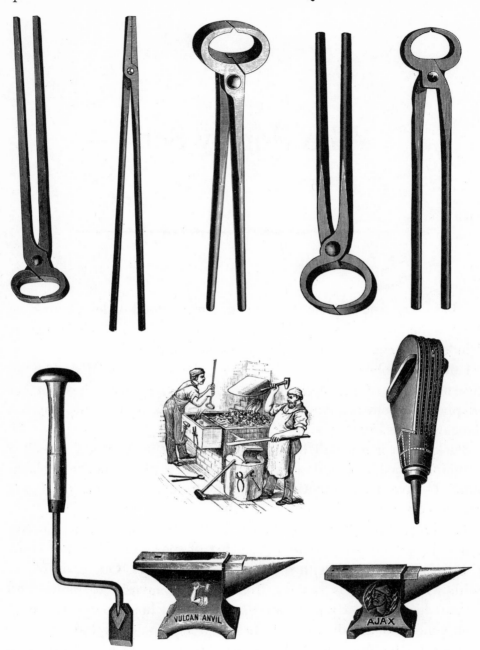

Here, surrounding a drawing of a blacksmith's forge, are adjuncts of his trade. Top row, from left: a cast-steel hoof nipper, blacksmith's wrought-iron tongs, and three pairs of steel pincers. A butteris (left) and a bellows (right) are on either side of the forge, with anvils on the bottom.

Blacksmith collectibles. Mule shoe at top left with two horseshoes below and drawing shoes at far right. Three Midway forges with cast-iron hearths are shown in the top row with a spiral-geared forge below at left and a blacksmith's blower to its right. Below these are a hot chisel (left) and a cold chisel (right). At bottom, from left, are a swage block, an angle-steel-frame blower, a set hammer and a flatter, and horseshoer's tongs just below them.

admire the work of the blacksmith, and I hope more of the artifacts he fashioned will be salvaged and appreciated in the coming years.

Blacksmiths permitted a golden opportunity for some measure of renown to slip through their fingers when they failed to sign their work. A very few did sign some pieces, but most of them were either too busy or too unlettered to undertake this chore. Occasionally you may encounter a signed Betty lamp or some other useful iron household article, and if you are a collector, this will be a happy occasion for you.

A good many iron objects one comes across these days have a pock-marked texture, and some persons believe this is a sign of great age and hand work. The case is quite to the contrary, I learned from reading a chapter devoted to the work of the blacksmith in Henry J. Kauffman's excellent book *Early American Ironware, Cast and Wrought,* published in 1966 by Charles E. Tuttle Company. This texture indicates a modern reproduction. The iron workers of years ago went all out to make their metal objects as smooth as possible.

Certain metal objects made by blacksmiths, and other categories of craftsmen as well, are now being collected, including early hinges, latches, and other hardware accessories, and such things as dippers, skimmers, and skillets. But there are tools of the blacksmiths' trade that deserve salvaging, and some of these could make neat conversation pieces for your home. They range from bellows to crimping tongs, from swage blocks to anvils.

It is unlikely that you will want to collect a great many blacksmith anvils unless you have a very stout floor indeed. But there is no reason why you should not seek out a few iron clippers, tongs, pincers and nippers, bellows, and even a small forge.

If you do find yourself enamored of anvils, try to locate a small one, weighing, say, about fifty pounds. One-hundred-pound anvils have been offered for sale of late at $25.00 or $35.00. A good old bellows may cost you $35.00 or $50.00, but for a few dollars each you should be able to pick up swage blocks (blocks with holes and grooves of different sizes and used for shaping metal articles difficult to work with on an anvil), crimping tongs (a pair was tendered recently for $6.00), and iron clippers.

Even early horseshoes are beginning to get scarce. I bought a few a couple of years ago for a dollar a pair.

Watch out also for such things as blacksmiths' hammers (the driving, hand, and rounding hammers were made in different shapes), butterises, and hoof nippers.

The blacksmith was sometimes called a farrier. A farrier made horseshoes, shoed horses, and also treated ailments that afflicted the horse.

A collection of handmade horseshoes themselves could be of major interest, because so many of them differed from others in size and contour. There were not nearly so many differences after the shoes began to be turned out by factories.

Some of our museums today have re-creations of the old-time blacksmith shop, and a trip through one, watching the operations that are performed there, can help round out the education of those who grew up after the horse-and-buggy days.

The illustrations accompanying this chapter will help identify a number of the collectible tools and adjuncts of the early trade of blacksmithing.

The best places to look for these things are in country barns and on farms which still have a horse or two around. Look for the run-down homes with a ramshackle barn out back while you're traveling around the countryside on a pleasant Sunday afternoon. You should be able to pick up horseshoes for less than a dollar and tools for not much more on erstwhile farms whose operators have taken jobs in nearby factories because of the difficulty of earning a livelihood these days on anything less than an estate-sized agricultural plot. Some country auctions offer good possibilities too.

Those interested will find an extraordinary collection of blacksmiths' and farriers' tools at the Shelburne Museum in Shelburne, Vermont. One will find there a Blacksmith and Wheelwright Shop that has preserved scores of tools of earlier years. Not long ago, H. R. Bradley Smith, assistant to the museum's curator, wrote a very fine book, *Blacksmiths' and Farriers' Tools at Shelburne Museum,* which constitutes a history of the development of these tools from the forge to the factory and which was published by the museum as Number 7 of its Museum Pamphlet Series. This is highly recommended to those who would like to become knowledgeable in this field.

A Rest for the Knife

FINE knife boxes have been collected through many decades, and the well-heeled can afford those of the Chippendale, Hepplewhite, and Sheraton periods. The knife rest—a far less expensive accessory of the dining table but one which once kept many a knife from spoiling the tablecloth—has a special appeal of its own and is available to those who collect on a limited budget.

The dining tables of our more affluent Victorian ancestors were brightened with knife rests of cut glass that sparkled brilliantly under the lights. Almost without fail, these were in the shape of miniature dumbbells—two balls joined by a barlike handle. But novelty knife rests, sometimes less expensive, were substituted for cut glass by the more adventurous of our great-grandparents who were not vitally concerned with keeping up with the more affluent Joneses.

Knife rests were made of silver, porcelain, pressed glass, wood, and Britannia metal.

The majority of knife rests measured from about three and a half to six inches in length, though a few shorter ones will be found. The height usually ranged from less than two to about three inches for those of cut glass but the novelty rests were often much higher.

Some small cut glass rests were available late last century for under $2.00 each, and even as late as the years just preceding the beginning of the First World War, excellent ones of this material were sold at retail for less than $5.00. Double that amount may get you one now,

The cut glass knife rests in the left column and bottom right date between 1907 and 1914. The squirrel rest is dated 1900, the swan rest, 1884, and the silver-plated rest below that is dated 1900.

and if you look long and hard enough, you may find some for $8.00 or $9.00.

It should go without saying that knife rests were utilized for keeping eating utensils that had been used off the dining table between courses, but eating habits have so changed that it is possible many collectors have never seen them. In today's formal and multi-coursed dinners, sufficient cutlery is usually placed on the table to avert the necessity for using the same implements for more than a single course.

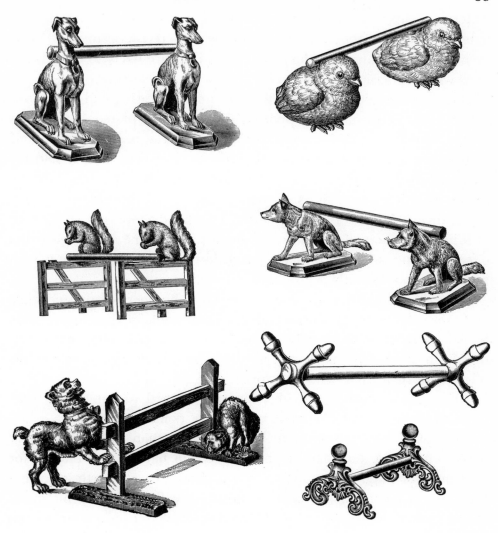

Novelty knife rests. Those in the top two rows are silver-plated and were being offered in 1892. The one at the bottom left was advertised in 1890, as was the one next to the bottom at right, which was silver-plated on white metal. The bottom rest at the right was available in 1905.

The traditional knife rest was either dumbbell-shaped, as in the case of those of cut glass and also of metal, or had a triangular section, but the novelty rests that became popular in the nineteenth century's waning years departed, sometimes radically, from these standards.

Many silver-plated rests were manufactured in unusual designs, some-times featuring animals and birds in their composition. Since good

American silver-plated wares of various types are now really beginning to attract the interest of those who were prone to pooh-pooh them not many years ago, the plated knife rests are likely to be pursued now with increasing avidity.

One popular rest in 1900 featured a squirrel on each end of the bar rest, which, in turn, was supported on miniature plated fence gates that resembled wood in appearance. This rest was two and a half inches long and about an inch and three quarters tall, and it sold for only slightly more than a dollar! In some rests the bar was held by swans, in others, by effigies of young boys.

Another type had a bar supported by plated embossed ends, each of which was actually made of a single piece of metal but gave the effect of being two curved pieces joined in the center. This type whole-saled in 1900 for only $.58 cents. (See illustration.)

Between 1900 and 1910, there were large numbers of pressed glass knife rests that sold for around a dollar each. Some of these were made by American glass factories but others were imported. These came primarily in clear glass. A crystal glass rest in the dumbbell shape was offered in 1907 at a wholesale price of $.40.

Silver-plated knife rests with supports attached to flat round bases were available about the same time at a dollar a pair.

Porcelain knife rests seem to be far scarcer than those of glass or metal, but one of porcelain in the blue Onion pattern was offered for sale some time ago at $5.50. You may find others well worth acquiring for under $10.00, though some of the finest will cost you a bit more.

Interesting novelty-type rests of plated silver will be encountered from time to time at prices of $5.00 to $10.00. A few dollars should purchase one of pressed glass, and some of pottery have been offered for $5.00 to $7.00.

Cut glass values are based on the size, pattern, and quality. Many of these were cut to match the patterns of services and some were even produced in a size large enough to hold a carving knife. Although the majority of cut glass rests were in clear glass, some were produced in colored glass and will fetch higher prices when they can be found.

Finally, country-made knife rests whittled of wood and rests of wire were used by some families that could not afford what to them was an extravagant expenditure for gadgets in earlier years, and you may, with luck, stumble across one of these in your peregrinations. Don't turn up that nose at them: they are much scarcer than the traditional types.

The regular antiques shops will be your best bet for the majority of knife rests, and you'll just have to shop around for the best prices. But if you can find them in good condition at the prices suggested above, you can probably make a good investment, because of the increasing interest in the smaller collectible objects.

Horseradish!

———————————◁◇▷———————————

WHEN I was much younger, the word "horseradish" was used as an exclamation to convey the same sense of incredibility as did "bologna," pronounced and often spelled "baloney." This colloquial usage has about run its course, for which horseradish addicts may be grateful.

I have never run across a fine collection of horseradish jars, simply because, I think, almost no one has thought much about them and no one has yet written much about them. The reason bride's baskets, for example, fetch as much as they do is not just because they are attractive and can grace one's living area but also because someone gave these berry bowls a catchy nickname and a number of articles have been written about them.

Little has been written about mustard jars, which are also delightful and which were produced in many charming forms and shapes through the years. Thousands of them were on the market during the early years of the present century in silver-plated holders, which—if one wanted to rescue a colorful word from oblivion—one could term "snazzy." Early manufacturers called these containers pots and also applied the same term to horseradish containers.

Both the horseradish and the mustard jars (or pots, if you prefer) were made of glass encased in fancy holders and also of metal and porcelain. There were attractive ones of plated silver with glass linings, usually round in shape. Whereas the mustard pots had lids, usually

Mustard and horseradish pots. Top row, from left: cut glass mustard and two cut glass horseradish jars, and a mustard pot in filigree silver-plated stand. Second row: mustard pot with silver-plated filigree, satin-cut plated mustard pot with glass liner, and silver-plated mustard pot with English grape decoration. Third row: horseradish pot with pierced silver plate, lunch caster with a glass mustard jar and lunch caster with mustard and horseradish pots. Bottom row: plated mustard pot in filigree holder, cut glass horseradish jar, glass horseradish pot in filigree holder, and silver-plated mustard pot with Sheffield Grape design. These date variously between 1884 and 1914.

with a handle attached, horseradish pots customarily had glass stoppers with bulbous tops.

According to Dr. Arthur G. Peterson's excellent book *Salt and Salt Shakers,* published in 1960, the use of ground mustard for seasoning began in England around 1720, although mustard seed were used in ancient times. Mustard containers came into widespread use in this country in the nineteenth century, he says.

The type available to the average collector today came into production in the eighteen-eighties. Some of these have flat lids; others boast domed ones with finials. Many caster sets of the type called lunch casters contained a mustard and a horseradish jar plus salt and pepper shakers, all held on a silver-plated base. E. G. Webster & Sons, one of the popular silver-plating companies, made a set of this type that wholesaled for $4.75 in 1913.

Homan Silver Plate Company, another widely known silver-plating firm, produced mustard jars in the Sheffield Grape design; the grapes were embossed on the jars.

Some exceptionally attractive holders for both mustard and horseradish pots were made in pierced patterns. These were extremely popular in the opening years of this century.

Naturally, scores of both types of jars were made in various patterns of cut glass. One finds these illustrated in numerous early trade catalogues, mostly at wholesale prices of under $5.00.

Novelty mustard containers were produced in pressed glass; and Dr. Peterson points out that beginning in the eighteen-eighties and for some years thereafter, mustard was sold in a variety of glass containers, some of them two-piece dishes of opaque glass with depictions of farm animals on their covers. Mustard also was marketed in pitchers with metal lids.

Mayonnaise jars and catsup containers apparently are of more recent origin, but you can collect a good many of these, too, if you wish.

You are likely to find the mustard, horseradish, mayonnaise and catsup containers on back shelves in some dealers' shops, because they have not yet attained the distinction accorded bride's baskets, tea caddies, and other table adjuncts, due largely to a lack of publicity about them. At most private home sales, they are not even put out with the other goodies, but if you'll inquire about them, you are likely to find them on pantry shelves or in kitchen cupboards and can probably acquire them at bargain prices. You'd also be well advised to check carefully through the advertisements in such publications as *The Antique Trader,* which constitutes the largest of all marketplaces for the newer collectible items.

The mustard and horseradish jars of pressed glass have been selling recently at prices of $1.00 to $15.00, with the majority of them in the $5.00 to $10.00 range. A footed glass globe that once contained mustard and sat upon a small nickel base was offered for sale within the past year at a dollar. You cannot find "sleepers" such as this every day, but you will find them occasionally if you'll keep your eyes open. And you should, if you set out right now before the word about them gets spread about, be able to amass a neat collection of mustard and/ or horseradish containers at an average price of less than $10.00 each. You can now find cut glass mustard jars in the shops for as low as $13.00 or $15.00, depending on the scarcity of the pattern. Be sure to check into the newer shops being opened by dealers who have not yet had much experience in selling antiques and who are likely to buy anything offered them for resale if the price is cheap enough. These dealers will catch on sooner or later; but at the outset, they are likely to have some bargains.

Marmalade is a word that simply has a high-priced sound, and if you ask an antiques dealer if he has a marmalade jar, you may find yourself confronted with one with a fairly high price tag on it. On the other hand, *mustard pot* is a homely phrase: the sound is a low-priced one. You may not think this is true, but it is—and the sounds of words and phrases have a psychological effect upon sellers and buyers alike. *Horseradish* is one of the homeliest of words; on the other hand, *honey jar* has a sort of velvety and therefore high-priced sound. Sometime when you have nothing better to do, talk to a psychologist or an expert in semantics about this sort of thing. Never use a fancy word when inquiring for a collectible item, if you can come up with a homely one instead.

If the idea of starting a collection of these intriguing little condiment containers we've been discussing appeals to you, then you may want to watch out for their companion spoons, resembling small ladles but occasionally with spadelike bowls. Some fine ones were manufactured in sterling silver and many others in plated silver. Rogers Brothers made silver-plated mustard spoons that wholesaled for $5.08 a dozen in 1900. It is interesting to note that this company's Lotus-pattern mustard spoon was offered for that price at the outset of the century but that the price of the same pattern had dropped to $4.70 in 1907.

Originally, a lot of the horseradish and mustard containers were offered together with a spoon. One of the former in a filigree-type silver-plated holder together with a spoon was priced at $2.10 wholesale in the 1890s.

Take a look at the illustrations to obtain an idea of the diversity of these pots.

If you don't want to follow the well-beaten path of the salt and pepper shaker collectors, horseradish and mustard jars (and spoons— or ladles, if you prefer) may be your dishes. Their pursuit can be great fun, and you should be able to accumulate a representative collection for an average expenditure of around $10.00 each or a bit more, excluding some of the scarcer cut glass ones.

I Fell Asleep Here...

——————————⊰◇⊱——————————

THE charming illustrations that adorn this chapter are those of bookmarks—a field that has been rather shamefully neglected by collectors, and particularly by those who don't read books. It is disheartening to have to point out that these include a large number of beginning collectors—the very individuals who should do the most reading.

The bookmark is not as popular today as it was early in the century, but using one to mark your place makes a lot more sense than turning down the page and damaging the book. I once had a friend who marked his place in books by inserting between their pages parts of sandwiches he had not completely devoured. This practice is even more deplorable than that of inserting between the pages a pair of shears, a cigarette lighter, or some other bulky object that can result in warping a book's covers when left there for a long period of time.

Literally scores of different types of bookmarks have been produced through the years, and they have been made of materials ranging from steel and silver to cloth and paper. I have had a few communications in recent years from individuals asking where they can obtain background about the early bookmarks—who designed and produced them, in what shapes they were made, and where they can be found. Some time ago I wrote a brief introductory essay to bookmark collecting for the magazine *Yankee;* but by and large, almost nothing will be found in print about the history of bookmarks. *Yankee* has been kind enough to permit me to include here a little of the background from my article.

The very earliest bookmarks may be traced back almost to the beginning of printing with movable type. These ancient ones were made primarily of parchment, though some also are believed to have been made of cloth and leather. They are just about as rare as copies of the Gutenberg Bible, which came off the press in 1455 or 1456 and which was the first book printed. Only forty-seven copies of this great milestone in our cultural history survive, and it is doubtful whether very many more bookmarks of parchment strips of around this same period can be found today.

Far more accessible are bookmarks dating from around 1850 to 1875, and those most easily obtained today (aside from those paper strips with advertising that continue to be published, and the modern bookmarks) are those turned out between about 1885 and 1920.

Some beautiful (and fairly costly) marks were manufactured of silver, and others of plated silver, but many more were made of silk, leather, cardboard, and paper. Nor should one pass by those quaint little crocheted marks that crop up now and then.

L. Prang and Company—a name associated primarily today with lithographs, greeting cards, and art materials—produced a large variety of charming lithographed bookmarks in its plant in Roxbury, Massachusetts. It was in 1866 that the German immigrant Louis Prang perfected the art of chromolithography—lithographic printing in various colors. Most bookmarks made by this firm probably date from around 1874, when the company went into the greeting card business.

Earlier bookmarks had been colored or painted by hand, and these are exceedingly scarce. (Some quite early ones were produced with the art of illumination, much of this work being attributed to monks in monasteries around the world.)

There are silk bookmarks available from before the mid-nineteenth century. The most famous of these are called Stevensgraphs and were woven on silk by the firm of Thomas Stevens in Coventry, England. This same company made a variety of other woven novelties on Jacquard looms. The bookmarks and novelties depict many subjects that Thomas Stevens found on old prints or in other sources, and a large number of them feature illustrations accompanied by verses.

Most Stevensgraphs are in the shape of oblong ribbons, ranging from an inch to about eight inches in width, with tassels at one or both ends. The bookmarks and other novelties impart a three-dimensional effect because of the depiction of figures of glossy threads against a flat and usually dull ground. The marks were commonly referred to as "ribbon pictures," and Stevens claimed to be the inventor of them. Most of the bookmarks were made after 1860, and they are becoming quite scarce and high-priced today.

In 1957, Wilma Sinclair LeVan Baker wrote an interesting book called *The Silk Pictures of Thomas Stevens*. Apparently issued in a fairly small edition, it is now out of print and when copies can be located, they will usually sell for $10.00 or more, although the book sold for $7.50 when first issued. It contains a number of fine illustrations of Stevensgraphs and is recommended to those interested in these extraordinary little ribbon pictures. Possibly you may find a copy of it in your public library. Mrs. Baker also wrote a brief article about Stevensgraphs that was published in the December 1962 issue of *The Antiques Journal*. It is possible that copies of this issue may occasionally be found in the stocks of dealers in back-issue magazines.

There was a firm in New Jersey, B. B. Tilt and Sons, that produced some rather similar bookmarks. Located in Paterson, the firm usually imprinted its name on its marks, many of which commemorated historical events or personages.

Woven or embroidered marks that look like miniature samplers are often enchanting and are especially desirable. Floral designs were the most popular for this type. Home artisans last century found ribbons available stamped with designs which they could embroider in colored threads themselves.

Bookmarks commemorating special events in the nation's history are highly collectible even though scarce. Many were printed on paper but others were made of such diverse materials as Celluloid (our first commercial plastic, perfected in 1866), leather, brass, silver, bone, and parchment.

As the nineteenth century grew toward a close, greeting card manufacturers turned to the production of bookmarks, many of them choice. In addition to Prang, these were produced by the firm of Raphael Tuck and others. Many featured satin ribbons. Still later, this type was made

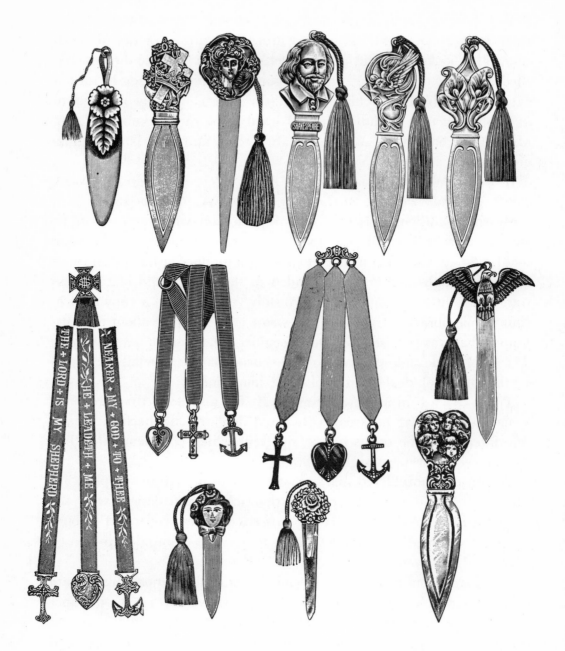

Silver and silk bookmarks and combination bookmarks and letter openers of the late nineteenth and early twentieth centuries. The two in the center of the second row were offered with either solid gold or sterling ornaments.

in the United States by Rust Craft, the well-known greeting card company of Dedham, Massachusetts. Some of the productions were of pierced, embossed cardboard, illustrated with scenes or figures.

The reason for the relative scarcity of these colorful cardboard markers today is that they were fragile and easily torn or destroyed.

Bookmarks of sterling silver began appearing late last century, and many of these had silk tassels attached. Many also had two-piece or pierced "blades" so they could be inserted around the page of a book. Hundreds of these were turned out in novel shapes and many were offered as combination bookmark-paper cutters. Handles were ornately embossed, and a number of these handles were in the shape of such things as fleur-de-lys, bumblebees, butterflies, leaves and grapes, sculpted heads, eagles, flowers (including one shaped as a single lily), and hearts. Depending upon how elaborate they were, these markers could be found early this century at wholesale prices from $.40 to about $3.00.

These silver and silver-plated bookmarks and combinations were manufactured in such profusion in earlier years that it is difficult to imagine where they have all gone, but a good many of them may still be found.

Also made in great abundance but becoming scarce because of their fragility are light cardboard or paperboard bookmarks with printed advertising on them. This type was particularly popular with book publishers, which placed them in copies of their new publications. This type usually contained advertising for one or more of the company's other new books. Because of the sudden surge of interest in all advertising mementoes of the past, you may very well find such marks, which have been available for a quarter or less, selling soon at substantially higher prices.

Not too many bookmarks were dated, but those bearing the dates of their issuance are desirable.

Although you may have difficulty locating desirable marks in the shops, you are apt to find a great many of them in the likeliest of places—inside old books, long ago placed there and forgotten by their owners. The next time you're in a shop featuring used books, try thumbing through the pages of some of them. It is certainly not inconceivable that you may find there bookmarks of greater value than the books themselves.

Though the Stevensgraphs may fetch $35.00 or more when they can be found, thousands of marks are available at much lower prices. A silk bookmark commemorating the visit of General Lafayette to the United States in 1824 was offered not too long ago at $18.00, and a rather similar commemorative one with no text, at $15.00.

A couple of years ago you could find excellent sterling markers at prices of $6.00 to $8.00, but these values are on the rise. A woven silk mark made by the firm of B. B. Tilt and featuring an American flag was tendered about a year ago at $9.00 but would be worth more now.

However, paper and cardboard markers are often encountered for $.15 to $.50, and silk ones at a dollar or so. If you're interested, you'd better rush out and try to gather a few, because prices will probably be up as soon as the delight and current inexpensiveness of collecting these reminders of a past day catch the attention of more people.

Open with Care

CALL the implements pictured in this chapter what you wish— letter openers, paper knives, or paper cutters. They have been called all these names through the years. We'll discuss them here because they are like the combination bookmark-paper cutters we talked about in the preceding chapter.

Letter openers—simple handled blades for the most part—are still in use today, but most of them simply can't hold a candle to the elaborate cutters of years past. Secretaries employ today's paper knives to open letters for their busy employers; but chances are that if their employers had an assortment of those fascinating knives of three quarters of a century or so ago, they'd open their own letters, just for the sheer joy of handling the cutters.

Of special interest (and increasing value) are paper knives with elaborately wrought sterling silver handles and either steel or pearl blades. These were turned out in an astonishing variety of shapes and sizes early in this century and were popular for at least the first two decades. There was little difference in price originally between comparable cutters with pearl blades and those with nickel-plated steel blades. Early twentieth-century trade catalogues offered them at wholesale prices of $4.00 to $18.00 a dozen, depending primarily on size. A seven-and-a-half-inch-long knife was offered with a steel blade at $12.00 a dozen, compared with $18.00 a dozen for the same knife with

Letter openers in varying sizes. The one across the top has a white pearl handle and was part of a desk set. Just below it is a combination letter opener and bookmark with an ornate sterling handle. The third from the top is one with an ivory blade, and there are ivory blades on the two bottom ones. The third one from the bottom has a pearl blade.

a pearl blade, but in smaller sizes, the price variation was very small indeed.

Delicate paper knives, popular with the ladies, were made in very small sizes, some less than four inches in length. As was the case with so many silver and silver-plated articles of the times, the handles of these cutters were decorated with such things as flowers, vines, geometrical designs, and beading. Many, too, reflected the early twentieth-century Art Nouveau influence.

Some blades were straight; some tapered to a point; and still others were scimitar-shaped. There were also oval blades that tapered to a point at the extremity.

Knives with silver-plated handles, of course, were far less expensive than those with handles of sterling. Many inexpensive desk sets were produced, frequently consisting of such letter-writing and letter-opening adjuncts as a blotter, pen, ink eraser, and letter opener. Some such sets sold for a very few dollars, and even cheaper ones were retailed on a piece of cardboard for less than a dollar.

In general, the same types of handles used on paper cutters were also attached to shoehorns, nail brushes and files, toothbrushes, shoe buttoners, cuticle knives, ink erasers, seals, and even curling irons.

The desk sets made early in this century were often intriguing because of the articles they contained. Benj. Allen & Company of Chicago offered for $4.70 wholesale in 1905 a set housed in a cloth-lined paper box and containing a paper knife, a penholder, a crystal ink bottle with a silver-plated top, a silver-handled rolling blotter, a seal, an ink eraser, and a crystal mucilage bottle. If you could find such a set intact today it probably would cost $30.00 to $40.00.

In 1914, the A. C. Becken Company, wholesale jewelers of Chicago, were offering letter openers with inexpensive sterling silver handles for as little as $.50 to $.70 each, indicating that the value of silver had risen little since the turn of the century.

Some letter openers were made with pearl handles and steel blades. Becken offered one set consisting of such a letter opener, plus an eraser and a seal, both with pearl handles, for $3.65. Openers also were produced with handles of ebony, Celluloid, and other materials.

In 1901, *The Youth's Companion,* which was probably more heavily involved in the premium business than any magazine of its day, offered to readers who turned in one subscription plus $.20 "one of our great offers of the year." The premium consisted of a paper cutter with a sterling silver handle and a pearl blade, and a penholder with a gold-plated mounting and a "solid gold" pen. We may assume that the word "pen" referred to the penpoint.

If you start collecting letter openers, you'll find they are available at a good many shops for a few dollars each. After you have assembled a good collection of them, you probably will start collecting inkwells. From there you will spread out to pens and penholders, letter seals, ink erasers, writing boxes, and lap desks.

So don't say you weren't warned.

A Pin in a Haystack

IT is just as easy to lose a pin in a haystack as it is to lose a needle in a haystack. I am not sure that this is one of the reasons that pincushions were invented, but it could have been. Haystacks have been around for a long time and so have pincushions.

How far back in time would you guess that the use of pincushions goes? If you guess a century, you will miss the answer by several centuries.

Pincushions date back at least to the reign of Queen Elizabeth I of England and Ireland, and she ascended the throne in 1558, which, even calculated by the new math, was more than four hundred years ago. Metal pins in those days were both scarce and costly, and it was imperative that some way be devised to keep them from disappearing. Chances are that little boxes for the safekeeping of these pins (some of them literally precious) were utilized before the advent of pincushions.

In 1911, Eleanor D. Longman and Sophy Loch wrote a charming book called *Pins and Pincushions*. It was published in London by Longmans, Green & Co., Ltd. and has long been unavailable except in establishments handling out-of-print and rare books. Most of this volume is concerned with pins, but there is a discussion of early pincushions near the close of the book. In this, the authors point out that our predecessors used "pin-poppets" in which to carry pins on their persons. Pin-poppets were containers with lids or stoppers, and they housed both pins and needles and could be carried about in one's pocket. They were made both of metal and wood and were oval in shape.

The authors do not venture to guess the age of the pin-poppets, but they conclude that boxes or cases of some kind were used to house pins even before the reign of Queen Elizabeth.

Collectible pincushions from the late nineteenth and early twentieth centuries.

Four centuries ago, pincushions were referred to as "pyn-pyllows," which translated into contemporary English is "pin-pillows." The reason they were so called is undoubtedly that the earliest pincushions actually were in the shape of miniature pillows. They were achieved through the art—and we use that word advisedly—of needlework.

The authors of *Pins and Pincushions* conclude, as a result of studious research in the field, that there was little change in the shape of these pillow-type pincushions for almost two centuries after Elizabeth's reign. They continued to be made of needlework, some with tassels at the corners and others with a lace or cord edging.

However, they added, late in the seventeenth century there appeared round pincusions covered with silver thread and with silver mounts. These were intended to be suspended from the waist.

Knitted pincushions date from the mid-eighteenth century, and these are quite scarce today; many of those that have survived are museum pieces, and are certainly worthy of such care.

In the early nineteenth century, the novelty pincushion appeared, and with the passing years it grew more and more novel until by late in the century they were about as novel as they could get. These are the ones you'll be looking for.

Large pincushions were put together for use on the dressing table or in the workbox, and smaller ones were fashioned for carrying on the person. Generally speaking, the homemade forms were fairly simple; but when the store-bought pincushions took over, there were some radical changes in design.

Needlework and ladies' magazines of earlier years frequently published designs for pincushions to be made at home, most of them simple in form but decorated with attractive designs in needlework. Some covers were made of canvas embroidered in colored silk; others were em- broidered with floral and other designs or with the initials of the owner. A good many of these homemade cushions were in pillow shapes; others resembled round balls; still others took the shape of hearts. Elaborate ones were sometimes decorated with beading.

Work baskets were made with large pincushion tops. There were novelty pincushions in the shapes of vegetables and fruits, including strawberries, apples, pears, pumpkins, and even carrots.

Popular in the 1890s were sets that included a pincushion and a couple of toilet bottles. The cushions were fabricated of heavy bolting cloth, and the bottles were covered in similar material. Often ribbon bows adorned the pincushions. The materials were hand-painted. Such sets wholesaled for $3.00 to $3.50 eighty years ago.

Quite popular, too, were pincushions of plush mounted on silver or silver-plated bases. The bases sometimes were footed and decorated in floral designs.

Scores of novelty cushions were produced in the 1890s and early 1900s. A favorite type was one designed in the form of a miniature shoe measuring six or seven inches in length. The shoe itself was made of silver plate or white metal and held the cushion in its top. Not long before the First World War this type could be purchased for as little as a dollar.

Dozens were made with velvet tops and enameled tubs or bases, and inexpensive types could be had for a quarter or so. They were produced as miniature replicas of animals (turtles, dogs, monkeys, bears, mice, birds), flowers, spiderwebs, hats and caps, vehicles, items of furniture such as stools and cradles, mittens, skates, and even grindstones.

Some of the unusual pincushions boasted sterling or silver-plated ornaments, often with tassels attached.

If you want a truly delightful field in which to collect without ending up in bankruptcy court, investigate pincushions. You'll find more commonplace types at prices of less than $5.00 each. You probably can find some for one or two dollars. The earlier ones may set you back $15.00 to $20.00.

Recently there have been offered for sale: a velvet pincushion with beading for $3.50; a small shoe pincushion for $6.00; a velvet cushion set in a miniature high-top shoe for $4.50; a heart-shaped one of velvet for $1.25; one of hand-crocheted satin for $1.00; and one in the shape of a cow's hoof for $4.00.

A varied assortment of pincushions looks nice on a whatnot, if you can stand whatnots.

A lot of pincushions are still around in older homes; and when a house sale is advertised at one of these, make it a point to inquire casually whether any may be available. They are not likely to be out with the porcelain, silver, and furniture that are being offered for sale; but some may be tucked away in a bedroom drawer or elsewhere in the house and the owner may be delighted to accept a dollar for them, unless you drool over them and thereby send the price up.

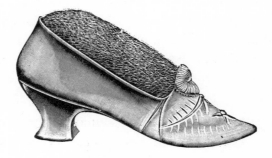

Pincushion in the shape of a shoe. These were made at various times from the 1880s through World War I.

Chances are, too, that your own grandmother may have one or two around, since grandmothers did a lot more sewing than their grand-daughters. Another likely place is the shop that acquires most of its inventory from private homes. Just a few days before starting to write this chapter, I picked up from one such shop a delightful quilted pincushion in varied colors for a dollar. It was bordered around the edges with twelve small cloth heads and is truly charming.

Full Measure

CHANCES are you've never thought of the prosaic tape measure as a collector's item. But not all tape measures were by any means prosaic. Our imaginative ancestors took care of that when they put their fertile imaginations to work on tape measure cases with eye appeal.

Three quarters of a century ago a tape measure case could actually be a piece of creative art, and this was particularly true of the small measures used as adjuncts of sewing.

Numerous designs were fashioned in silver or silver-plated cases, and, like the pincushions discussed in the preceding chapter, they frequently took novelty forms. Some were in the shape of animals (turtles and fish), straw hats, and human heads.

Most of these small cases contained a yard of tape, although some smaller ones were produced with only two feet. A good many of the cases were engraved or otherwise decorated in rococo designs or with quaint or amusing depictions of individuals or scenes.

Quite cheap cases were produced in white metal. One popular type of these was in the shape of a straw hat and was lettered with the words "Most hats cover the head, this covers the feet." That was quite a pun in 1900.

Puns were featured in the lettering of other cases also. One depicted a yard filled with individuals outside a house. Below this scene was the phrase "A Full Yard."

Tapes in novelty cases of sixty to seventy years ago.

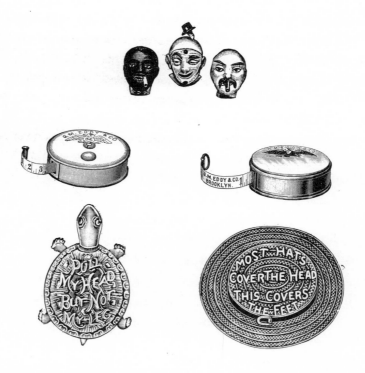

Unusual tape cases together with a standard G. M. Eddy & Company
steel tape (at right center).

There was one case showing a woman's two feet and one foot of a man. The accompanying phrase was "Three Feet."

Other cases were decorated with the traditional floral and geometric motifs so popular at the turn of the century.

Most of these cases were the so-called self-winding types. In addition to the sewing tapes, there also were other types in interesting decorated cases, including nickel-plated carpenter's pocket tapes. The tapes themselves were of steel. One widely sold type was manufactured by G. M. Eddy of Brooklyn, New York, who also produced a plastic case in the 1880s, only fifteen years or so after the perfection of our first successful commercial plastic, Celluloid.

The width of the tapes themselves generally ranged from one-fourth to one-half inch, although some measured five eights of an inch in width.

In addition to metals and plastics, cases were made of leather of various types, including ass skin.

Because there is no such organization yet as an association of tape collectors and because there is virtually no literature available about the early tape measure cases, there are no standards by way of prices. You know, of course, you'll have to pay more for a measure in a sterling silver case then one in a steel or leather case. You'll also have to search about for them, since they have not as yet appeared—certainly in any quantity—in antiques shops. But the search may be worth it. You should be able to pick up some of these cases from homes for a pittance, and when the fact becomes bruited about that here is a fascinating little gadget well worth collecting, you'll be glad you did.

If you want to, you can even establish and elect yourself as first president of the American Association of Measuring Tape Collectors.

The Flower Children

―――――――――――⟨◇⟩――――――――――――

I F there was anything our late-Victorian ancestors loved more than
flowers, it was vases to display them in.

It would require a huge catalogue merely to picture each of the different types of vases produced between 1885 and 1901. It was in the
latter year that Victoria ended her sixty-three-year-old reign, thereby
bringing to a close one of the most fantastic eras in the history of
production and design.

The late years of the Victorian era saw not only the revival of earlier
styles but an indiscriminate mingling of them—a practice loudly de-
cried by twentieth-century critics, who only during the past few years
have mellowed a trifle, realizing, at last, that there is really nothing
horrendous about mixing styles in decoration and that, in fact, this
practice can lend color, variety, and interest to the contemporary home.

Interest in so-called classicism was manifested at various periods during the Victorian years, and there was some revival of this interest in
the late part of this period. One evidence of this interest is found in
the designs of many vases of the late nineteenth and very early twentieth
centuries. One example was the popularity of the cornucopia vase.
The cornucopia, you'll recall if you know anything at all about ancient
mythology, was the fabulous horn of a noble she-goat named Amalthaea,
which suckled the god Zeus. Through the centuries that horn has been
represented as overflowing with fruit, flowers, and the good things of
life and has been adapted for use by thousands of designers of scores

On the top row are vases of crystal glass (second and third from left), cut glass (left and fourth from left), and silver plate. At the extreme left in the center row is a ruby glass holder in an elaborate silver-plated base. To its right are a card stand with vase attached, a 1900 silver-plated base with glass holders, and a silver-plated vase. In the bottom row: a vase and a rose bowl, both of cut glass, a Homan silver-plated vase, and a hand-painted porcelain vase.

While they were not issued during the Brilliant Period (which ended, for the most part, about 1905), these 1914 cut glass vases are not to be sneezed at. Nor were they originally inexpensive. Some of those shown here wholesaled for as high as $50.00 to $100.00 apiece, although most were priced lower. Not many people are familiar with the manufacturers' original names which follow. Top row, from left: Elenore, unnamed, Alhambra, and Madeline. Bottom row, from left: Victory, Peacock, Chester, Ethel, and Plaza.

of objects in many lands. It has been a motif in furniture decoration in particular, from the Renaissance to modern times and was a favorite stencil design last century. A favorite American sofa in the Empire style boasted cornucopia, or horn-of-plenty, designs carved on its back, arms, and legs.

Many, though not all, late nineteenth-century cornucopia vases were made of glass inserted in a metal horn, customarily supported on a metal base. Because our Victorian ancestors loved color, the glass was frequently ruby in color. In fairly inexpensive vases of this type, the metal was plated silver.

The cornucopia is one of scores of types of Victorian vases that can be collected today by individuals with limited bank accounts.

One advantage in collecting vases, of course, is the fact that they can be utilized today throughout one's home for their original purpose of holding flowers and vines. Some of them even look good with artificial flowers, so that if you like, you can have gorgeous red roses in your living room in mid-December.

The purpose of this chapter is primarily to suggest some of the varied types of vases of our recent past that can be purchased inexpensively and whose values are likely to climb in the years ahead.

Naturally, you will not find many of the aristocratic cut glass vases of our Brilliant Period in the junk shops, though you may encounter some in the better pawnshops, because they are now considered excellent collateral for a loan. But you are likely to find in the junk shops numerous pressed and blown glass vases, many of them in metal holders, and you may even occasionally find there vases of porcelain with much to commend them.

Art glass vases of the types now so avidly collected, ranging from Mother-of-Pearl satin glass to cameo glass, are expensive, but not nearly so expensive are hundreds of vases in both clear crystal or colored pressed and blown glass and in hand-painted porcelain that flooded the market between 1890 and 1915. They are horn-shaped, bulbous, squatty, avoid, round—you name the shape and you're likely to find it somewhere. Many of the newer antiques shops are running over with such vases priced at just a few dollars each. Generally speaking, good colored glass will bring a higher price than clear, although this is not invariably the case.

Thousands of conical-shaped vases were produced with metal holders or stands. Some of the latter were quite sedate in character but many were both fancy and fanciful. In fact, some manufacturers referred to their wares as "fancy vases."

Many holders were either in the shape of or were decorated with cast figures of cupids or scantily clad children and some were adorned with scantily clad figures of adults, often females with bare breasts (a novelty in those days).

A large number of vase stands late last century and early in this one were bronzed or gilded or made of ormolu, which is an alloy of copper and zinc used to imitate gold (or gold prepared for use in gilding).

There was a revival of naturalistic design in vases, with both glass and metal fashioned in the shape of leaves, and some were molded as stylized flowers—a characteristic of the Art Nouveau influence.

Many vases were made in pairs, though it is becoming increasingly difficult to find the original pairs intact today, because of separation and breakage through the years.

Carloads of enameled or painted glass vases were also turned out, and unless you are a pretty fair artist yourself, you will want to buy only those whose enameling or paint remains in good condition. Thousands of enameled ceramic vases also were manufactured.

Vases of the type called "Mary Gregory" were made both in this country and abroad. This glass was most often enameled with figures of children. This type of glass is named, as almost everyone now knows, after a decorator named Mary Gregory, who is said to have worked in the decorating department of the Boston & Sandwich Glass Company.

Large quantities of this same type of enameled vase (usually featuring tinted faces) were imported from Bohemia and elsewhere. The Mary Gregory glass made at the Boston & Sandwich works is reputed to have been devoid of tinting. Early Mary Gregory vases and other pieces are going up in price, and the collector should know that this type of glass is now being reproduced, so unless she is an expert herself, she should buy only from reputable dealers.

Satin glass has been popular for many years, and vases of satin glass are still available in large quantities. They are not extremely costly but, depending on type and quality, may set you back $35.00 to $75.00 or more. These were produced in plain colors, shaded colors, and with various types of decoration. Early satin glass vases also are now being reproduced.

Ruby glass, popular in the 1890s and early 1900s, is a flashed glass with a thin coating of color over clear glass. Simple vases in this were quite inexpensive some years ago, and they may still be bought at very reasonable prices, although values have been ascending somewhat of late because of the revival of the popularity of colored glass. Here once more there is a reproduction problem.

All types of vases have been made through the years with applied glass decoration in various forms, particularly in the shape of leaves, berries, and fruits. Some of these are quite attractive and interesting, and many of those of earlier years are still plentiful in a price range of $15.00 to $45.00 and $50.00.

Greatly abundant are those translucent types of white vases commonly called "Bristol" and made from about 1870 on. This should not be confused with the fine enameled glass that was produced in England in the eighteenth century and that acquired the name Bristol, whether made in the city of that name or in English glasshouses elsewhere. The later Bristol glass was a much cheaper product and was made in and shipped out of Bohemia in great quantities. It also was made elsewhere, including the United States. It was fairly cheap originally and vases of this type may be found today in scores of antiques shops at prices of $15.00 to $35.00, with some of the larger ones with quality enameled decoration valued higher.

These so-called Bristol vases should be judged primarily on the quality of their decoration and should not be bought indiscriminately merely because they have been designated Bristol vases and have acquired some age. Some of them bear evidence of having been enameled by amateurs, but some of these are quaint and attractive. Others are decorated with professional skill.

Overlay vases, made of two or more layers of glass with cutting through one or more layers, are frequently attractive and worth acquiring. Here again the beginner will encounter difficulty in distinguishing those made half a century or more ago from those being produced today. If he continues to handle as much of this type of glass as possible, views as much of it as he can in museums and other collections, and devotes some time to reading about it in the numerous books that deal with glass, he will eventually come to get what collectors and dealers call, for want of a better word, the "feel" of it.

In making overlay glass, the base color is usually white or clear and the other layers, red, rose, amber, and so on. Overlay vases were made by glasshouses in the United States, England, France, and Bohemia last century. During the last thirty years of the nineteenth century a cheaper type of glass that imitated overlay was made. Vases of this type were blown and treated to produce effects similar to overlay. A polka-dot pattern is frequently encountered in imitation overlay.

Fine early overlay vases were not cheap; but unless the flood of reproductions discourages collecting, their values are destined to rise. They were made when labor was far cheaper than it is now.

Vases with splotches of color called Spatter glass and those with various colors and the addition of mica flakes or aventurine, called Spangled glass, are intriguing and were produced by many glasshouses here and abroad. Recently they have been coming out of Czechoslovakia. Some dealers lump these together and call them "End of Day" glass. Strictly speaking, "End of Day" should be applied to certain offhand pieces done by glass blowers to use up small batches of glass left in the furnace pots after the end of the day's work. Neither Spatter nor Spangled glass was made this way, but constituted regular production items sold to the trade.

Depending on size and decoration, Spatter glass vases are available at prices of from $18.00 to $50.00. Spangled glass usually brings a bit more—from around $35.00 to $75.00 for a choice specimen.

We'll not concern ourselves here with the higher-priced types of art glass vases, since they are outside the scope of a book dealing with poor man's antiques.

Ceramic vases were turned out by all the leading porcelain and pottery plants as well as by many you have never heard of and probably never will hear of. Once more, these should be judged on the quality of their work. Quantities of hand-painted porcelain vases that retailed from $2.00 to $15.00 were made early in this century. Those impressed with the marks of well- and favorably known potteries may bring premium prices, but if you're a good judge of design and quality, you can frequently pick up fine unmarked porcelain vases for little or nothing more than their original selling prices. The reason for this is that so many collectors pay for "names." In a way, this is a pity, because some generally poor productions came out of many big-name factories. This is as true of some Meissen pieces as it is of pieces made in smaller and lesser-known factories. American's Rookwood Pottery last century made many gorgeous vases, but now and then one will encounter quite mediocre work with the Rookwood mark.

This chapter is intended merely to bring the matter of vases of collectible age and merit to your attention. You will find excellent discussions of the types of materials of which these vases were made in dozens of good books available, some of which are listed in the bibliography of this book. By all means consult these if you want to collect vases (or other similar objects of glass or metal).

This chapter's illustrations will serve to give you an indication of the really tremendous variety of sizes and designs in which vases were made sixty-five to 100 years ago. One thing's for sure: if you decide to collect vases, you'll never encounter a serious shortage of them, even though the prices of the better types will probably go up within the next few years.

Tea for Two

—◦◦◦—

A LOT of Americans, imitating the English, collect early tea caddies, which is just fine with me. But I have been wondering of late why so few are collecting other perfectly fascinating accessories of tea making and tea drinking. I am a coffee man myself, but I find myself greatly intrigued by such genteel accessories as sterling silver tea balls, tea strainers, and, of course, tea bells. One can even collect the tin canisters and tin cans of earlier days in which bulk tea was sold.

You need only glance at the illustrations accompanying this chapter to see what I mean. There are various shortcuts to tea making today, and we use them when we are in a hurry. But brewing tea with the use of sterling or even silver-plated tea balls should, I think, be something of a ceremony, to be indulged in on a lazy day when there are no immediate chores confronting you and you have the leisure to sip and savor your tea instead of quaffing it as you do your morning coffee when you are rushing to catch the train, the subway, the taxi, or whatever conveyance speeds you to your workaday chores.

Perforated sterling or silver-plated tea balls were made in various sizes to hold varying amounts of tea leaves, depending upon the quantity you intended to brew. They were round or oval and were linked by a chain to a ring by which they could be lifted from the pot or the kettle when the proper time arrived.

The tops of the tea balls could be lifted so the tea could be inserted inside. The bubbling water flowed through the ball's perforations, which

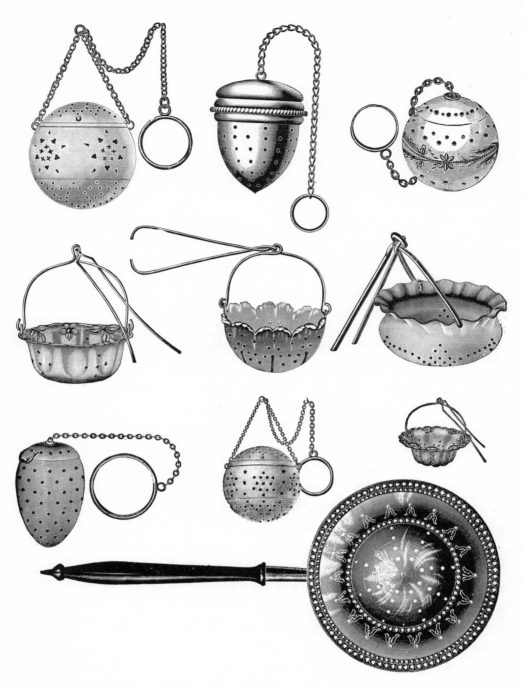

A strikingly handsome group of silver and silver-plated tea balls and strainers offered for sale between 1900 and 1908.

Tea bells with decorated handles. Art Nouveau influence is seen in the handle at top left. The stork at right was advertised early in this century. The bell second from the left at the top has a stag-horn handle and the one at the bottom right has a handle of ebony. The others are of sterling silver or silver plate.

sometimes were in designs of stars and crosses and even hearts, much like some of the Pennsylvania Dutch pierced tinware. Though the majority of these tea balls were round, some were egg-shaped. Moreover, some of them were engraved with simple but rather attractive designs.

In 1900, elegant silver-plated tea balls sold at wholesale prices of $2.50 to $3.50, and the wholesale prices of those of sterling were only $4.00 or $5.00.

Whereas the shapes of tea balls were quite limited, those of tea strainers were varied indeed. Some were fabricated as small, round bowls with perforated sides and bases and were held by a metal prong; others were oval, square, or oblong with handles. Some handles were made of sterling silver; some of plated silver, and still others of wood, notably ebony. A number of them had a metal prong on the top surface opposite the handle, by which they could be rested on a receptacle.

The more expensive strainers were engraved or embossed or had pierced-work extensions around their tops. In 1908, sterling strainers of this kind were wholesaling at prices ranging from about $4.00 to $6.00 or more. Wholesale prices of some of the delightful silver-plated ones in 1900 were as little as $1.25. By 1914, this same type had increased to only $1.35. Inflation had not quite set in. If you had a friend who could get it for you wholesale, you could buy a truly fine handled and silver-plated tea strainer in 1914 for $3.00.

Tea bells, while normally small, came in almost as many designs as vases, but not quite. A great many bell collectors seek fine tea bells, but a lot of these are still around, because their tinkle in earlier times was not limited to summoning family or guests to tea, but to meals as well, and they were sometimes pressed into service (as they still are) by invalids who needed or wanted some attention.

The most intriguing thing about tea bells is their handles, most of which were richly (and often extravagantly) decorated. Most popular were floral motifs. The tea bells, as were the balls and strainers, were made in both sterling silver and plate. It seems incredible that some small ones with fine sterling handles were retailing just sixty years ago for only about a dollar. Extra-fine ones might have cost you $2.00. Lovely tea bells also were made in rich cut glass and sold for more, originally, than those of sterling.

For those with limited space and limited funds, tea balls, strainers, and bells offer a fertile opportunity. There are so many bell collectors around now that they have run the price of fine bells up somewhat. This does not mean the prices are now exorbitant or that the available supply is nearing exhaustion. A few dollars will get you a nice silver-plated bell, but those of cut glass will cost you a good bit more. And the cut glass ones are worth it; you are not apt to see their like again.

Elephants Had Them Too

THIS is probably as good a place as any to throw in a few words about early trunks. The do-it-yourself craze is rapidly thrusting these old pieces of luggage to the forefront of avidly sought and somewhat oversized mementoes of the past.

Ladies with spare time on their hands and the creative urge buzzing within their breasts take these trunks and exercise upon their exteriors their own talents with paintbrush or stencil. In fact, many of the big trunks of last century have been converted into attractive and decorative storage areas by those handy with a brush.

We don't use nearly so many trunks today as our grandmothers and grandfathers did, and those we do use are chiefly smaller than many turned out in the nineteenth century. They also are simpler. The old ones often had special compartments for such things as hats, and trays of various sizes for special garments and other items of wearing apparel. Some even had "secret" compartments that were difficult to open unless one had knowledge of how they worked. Some of the trays were "automatic" and were lifted up and held in position by levers and gadgets.

Some inside tops were decorated with pictures, but quite often our forebears lined the insides of their trunks with newspapers, which will help date them.

Trunks were covered with leather, imitation leather, and canvas. A large number had polished brass trimmings of one sort or another and were hand-riveted to impart sturdiness. They were frequently bound around the outside by hardwood slats and were held together with heavy bolts and dowels. There were some companies years ago that specialized in manufacturing trunk hardware, one of the better known being J. H. Sessions & Son of Bristol, Connecticut. The hardware was made primarily of steel.

You can use the old trunks to store a thousand and one things in, from linens and blankets to clothing and geegaws. Restoration of those that have been badly used will take some work, but it can be pleasant. If the trunk is coated with paint as so many were, a good paint remover should be used. If the inside of the trunk is lined with early newspapers, you may prefer to let these remain as an indication of age. If it is lined with fabric that has become worn and dirty, you can simply strip this out.

If the trunk's exterior is rough and splintered, it will need to be

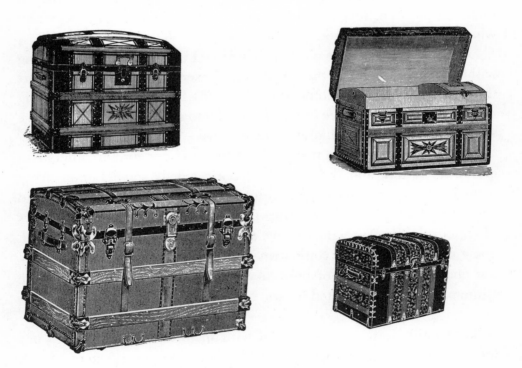

There's an increasing interest in old trunks for decorating. The two at the top and the one on the right at the bottom were available in 1892, the one at the lower left is dated 1889.

sanded well before applying a primer coat, which will seal the wood as well as prime it. This will need to be sanded after it has dried. Then, if you wish, buy yourself an antiquing kit and go to work. Most all of these come with directions for application.

Decoupage, an art that dates back quite a few years, is being revived now, and you might want to investigate the possibilities of decorating it by this method, or with stencils.

So many persons are now exhibiting an interest in restoring these trunks of an earlier day that books of decorating instructions have recently been published. If you're interested, turn to our bibliography.

You may still be able to practically steal trunks from old homes, but so many persons are now engaged in this slightly nefarious activity that there may be few left by the time this book reaches you. On the other hand, trunks are moving into antiques shops in increasing quantities, and the prices are going up. Recently, an eighteenth-century dome-top trunk with brass studs and measuring 29½ inches long and 14½ inches in width was offered for sale at $50.00 It was made of pine and had been refinished. Another eighteenth-century trunk covered with original hide was tendered at $20.00. A small leather-covered trunk with a large brass lock was priced at $12.50. I have seen other trunks in recent months at prices ranging from $5.00 to $75.00.

When the Lights Go Out

NOTHING comes in handier when your electric power suddenly fails at night than a candle. That is particularly true, I have learned, if you live in a rural area and it takes the repair crews a bit of time to reach your home and set things straight again.

At our house we no longer worry too much about power failures, because we have a good stock of candles, a supply of canned heat so we can make coffee, electricity or not, and a nice collection of candleholders so we won't have to tote the candles around the house by hand.

Novelty candleholders, including candelabra, offer an excellent opportunity for an attractive collection that can be both decorative and useful. Those of sterling silver are too rich for the blood of some of us, but those of plated silver, glass, or ceramics can often be accommodated by limited budgets.

Nearly all the silver-plating companies of years ago produced candlesticks and candelabra.

You will probably want a few candlesticks and candelabra in restrained designs, but if you are interested in assembling an unusual collection, investigate the novelty types that were manufactured in great abundance at the turn of the century. These were plated in both silver and gold and some of them had more convolutions than a snake tied in knots.

The silver-plating firm of E. G. Webster & Sons offered an Art Nouveau candelabrum in 1907 that featured a figure of a female clad in diaphanous raiment, with arms stretched above her head, clasping a part of the base of the affair, which also rested atop her head. It reminds you of the pictures you see of Atlas supporting the world on his shoulders. Five branched candleholders stem outward from the base on curved arms. This wholesaled originally at $7.75, but you could find the same design with four holders for $6.40 and with only three holders for $5.00.

Gold-plated candelabra and two silver-plated candlesticks, all made early in this century. The one top center is in the Art Nouveau tradition. Below are two candelabra, heavily plated.

Similar maiden figures were used for other candelabra as well as for individual candlesticks.

The branches of arms of virtually all the novelty candelabra were made in curved forms, some quite tortuous. Large numbers were decorated with applied ornament or by grooving or reeding. It is interesting to note that clock producers frequently offered clocks with a set of two candelabra; a great many of these were offered around 1905 to 1910 by Seth Thomas, Waterbury, and Gilbert in particular. With one of these on each side of the clock and the candles burning brightly, you had little difficulty in ascertaining the time.

Cast figures of cupids and angels all too often graced these clock-candelabra sets. There is nothing wrong with either cupids or angels per se; they have been used as art motifs for centuries. But some of those supporting, standing atop, pushing, or climbing upon the early twentieth-century candelabra and candlesticks possess such vapid expressions that one doubts their ability to pull a bowstring and flap those wings and soar. Moreover, some of the bare and semi-bare maidens look as if they had just emerged from the clothes wringer or a hard night's work scrubbing floors.

Many of these figured candleholders and candelabra were put on the market in the early years of this century by the M. S. Benedict Manufacturing Company of East Syracuse, New York, which also manufactured numerous other novelties now collectible. A large proportion of its output of candleholders, apparently, featured twenty-four-karat ormolu gold plate, hand-burnished.

Some of the Benedict candelabra bases were cast as figures that resembled a cross between a dolphin and an oversized chameleon. I have gone over some of these with a magnifying glass but am unable to identify the figures. Another holder was made in the shape of a maiden, bare except for a garland of leaves, standing upon an ornate base and supporting a candle cup in each of her upraised hands.

A rather quaint and somewhat interesting candlestick has a small cast figure of an elf at its base. There were some squat candlesticks on low square and footed bases that probably were used interchangeably for inkwells.

Saucer-shaped candlesticks or holders that had been utilized many years earlier were revived late last century with the saucers in the

At the top are two gold-plated candlesticks on either side of a silver-plated one. Center row, from left: silver-plated stick, a novelty gold-plated one, and a small rococo taper holder. Two interesting candlesticks are shown at bottom, the one at right, with a snuffer attached.

shape of leaves and with small carrying handles. Some had snuffers attached.

One candlestick of about 1905 that perplexes me is a representation of a child holding a candle cup aloft in one hand. The child apparently is wearing diapers and has what looks like a tourniquet high on its left arm. I am sure the tourniquet must have been affixed for some purpose, but for what purpose, I am unable to state.

Both attractive and relatively inexpensive are small ladies' taper holders, with a candlestick attached to a flat, oblong base with a handle. These were produced in both silver and silver plate.

Waterbury made some rather elaborate candelabra that could be had in either a gold or a "Venetian green" finish; the latter was more expensive than the former ($3.20 wholesale for one that was twelve and a quarter inches high and nine inches wide). Waterbury also produced some with columns of onyx.

In an 1884 catalogue, B. F. Norris, Alister & Company, a large wholesale jewelry firm, illustrated a silver five-light candelabrum with small shades atop conical holders. The wholesale price was $24.50—a fraction of what a replacement would cost today.

Some candelabra were combined with oil lamps, the latter fitted with porcelain shades. Some of these had cut glass oil reservoirs in colors and came complete with fancy candles.

Rococo decoration was in great demand on these lighting devices in the 1890s as will be evident in some of the illustrations.

Because of their great diversity of sizes, ornamentation, and materials, candlesticks and candelabra will be found in a wide range, but many should be available for less than $25.00 and many others for from $30.00 to $50.00.

In a kindred category are lusters, which are candleholders usually ornamented with cut glass pendants. Many of these are lovely but the better ones are fairly expensive and we will not be concerned with them here.

Candlesticks and candelabra are things to watch out for at estate dispersals and small-town auctions. The big-city auctioneers know the values of the costly ones all too well. If you visit the shops operated by the Goodwill Industries and kindred organizations that provide work for the handicapped, you'll be surprised at how often these lighting adjuncts will turn up at quite low prices. Often, these pieces are given to the Salvation Army, and it may pay you to cultivate the Salvation Army officials in your community, letting your wants be known: many collectors do and so also do dealers.

Newcomers to the antiques retail business sometimes pick up slightly damaged candlesticks and candelabra, which they offer at below-market prices. Often these can be repaired at a relatively small cost, and they are worth watching out for. You will not find many bargains in silver pieces at the better shops; but even at going prices, the silver ones could prove an excellent investment.

An intriguing Art Nouveau candlestick, ca. 1905.

Polly Wants One

―――――――――――――――◁◇▷―――――――――――――――

FEW receptacles have ever been more delightful than the late nineteenth-century cracker jars (the English call them biscuit boxes
and we use them today for cookies and call them cookie jars).

The loveliest of the cracker jars were made of glass with metal tops
and bails, or handles. Others were fashioned of porcelain, pottery, metals, and wood. A large number of English biscuit boxes were made
of silver plated on Britannia metal.

The cracker jar is a prime example of a utilitarian object that can
also be beautiful, and this applies especially to jars made of satin glass
and other types of art and decorated glass. These types are not being
given away today; some will bring $50.00 to $75.00 and even more.
But there are many that can be found with a bit of patience for less
than $50.00; and I have seen more recent types made of wood and
metal priced from $15.00 to $35.00.

Cookie jars, from the standpoint of being both useful and decorative,
bear kinship with certain types of cigar jars, ginger jars, and tea caddies.
In fact, I have seen exactly the same jar advertised in one publication
as a cookie jar and in another as a tobacco jar.

Enameled ruby glass cracker jars with silver or silver-plated lids and
bails were plentiful about seventy years ago, nor were those of decorated
satin glass very scarce; but they are becoming scarce these days because of the fascination they hold for collectors. The prices at which
some of these were offered some decades ago may upset you ($3.50 to

$6.oo), and you need not expect to find any at what seem such ridiculously low prices now; but you must remember about inflation and all that sort of thing. A few years ago some satin glass cracker jars were offered at $35.oo and even a little less, but they will bring about $5o.oo up today.

To get back to *The Youth's Companion* mentioned in an earlier chapter, this esteemed periodical about sixty-five years ago listed a charming cracker jar of German procelain as a premium in exchange

The cracker jar at top left has a decorated green bowl; the one on the right is of decorated porcelain and the center one is silver-plated. The second one from the left on the bottom row is of pink quilted satin glass. The two at right were characterized originally as either cracker or tobacco jars.

for one new subscription and $.30 additional for packing and postage.

Large numbers of these cookie or cracker jars were made by glass-houses around this country and abroad, and others were produced by noted potteries. An attractive fluted glass jar with a glass lid and finial was sold at $2.25 wholesale in 1905 by Benj. Allen & Company of Chicago. It measured nine and a half inches in height. This same company offered one in decorated opal glass with a silver-plated lid and bail at $3.45, and this one should bring around $45.00–$55.00 in the shops right now.

Some potteries turned out containers in porcelain and pottery for decoration by purchasers in their homes. Some of those obviously decorated by amateurs are quite respectable in appearance, but others indicate that their owners were practicing on them. Should you acquire one of the latter and desire to exercise your own artistic talents on its exterior, try using a good paint remover to take off the old decoration.

These jars, once filled with delectable tidbits, were made in all sorts of shapes—round, oval, square, bulbous and squatty, paneled, swirled, and so on. The smallest stood about six inches high, but a few ranged up to a foot tall. Many of the bails were elaborately decorated with engraving, embossing, and applied ornamentation.

Quite desirable are Wave Crest cookie jars made by blowing in full-size molds by the C. F. Monroe Company. Some of these now will bring $80.00 or more, Wave Crest wares of all types having caught the collector's fancy.

Very cheap cracker jars were once made of tin, but early tinware is now collectible. Even so, you may be able to find some of these for relatively few dollars.

Many of these containers were made by the potteries of France's famous Limoges district and are well worth acquiring, particularly if you can find them for around $25.00 or less. It should be pointed out, however, that porcelain with the marks of Limoges factories (of which there were and still are many) is rising in value. (The early Haviland factories were located in Limoges in the nineteenth century, but don't make the mistake of thinking that all Limoges china is Haviland china —or that all Haviland china was made in Limoges. Some of the latter was produced in the United States.)

A lot of the porcelain cookie jars did bear the name or mark of the factory that made them. To identify the producer, you should consult a book of pottery and porcelain marks. One of the best recent ones is Ralph M. and Terry H. Kovel's *Dictionary of Marks—Pottery and Porcelain*. Others include *Handbook of Old Pottery and Porcelain Marks* by C. Jordan Thorn; *Porcelain & Pottery Marks* by Urban Hartman; and *A Dictionary of Marks—Ceramics, Metalwork, Furniture,* edited by Margaret Macdonald-Taylor. A large part of the fun of collecting lies in identification of what one has acquired.

You will find some cookie jars in so-called "RS Prussia" china, made last century by the firm of Reinhold Schlegemilch, but there is an RS Prussia boom on right now, and to acquire one of these containers you may have to go without a few meals or maybe skip paying the rent for a month.

Hand-painted cracker jars in Japanese Nippon porcelain were made in some quantity, and you can probably pick up some bargains in these, because Nippon is moving into the collectors' market. Some of these have been available recently at around $15.00, but they probably won't be for much longer.

Many inexpensive squat cookie jars were made in German factories, and some of these are around at prices of under $25.00. Milk-white glass jars are not yet expensive either.

There were some English biscuit boxes made with a canister-like top on a footed base. Hand-painted biscuit boxes were made of Royal Worcester china with mountings plated on nickel silver. Somewhat similar ones were made in Coalport china and by Wedgwood and other noted English potters. Some had bail handles, others, tops with finials, and some were made of glass mounted in electroplated frames.

There were some charming English folding biscuit boxes in fancy designs, rather resembling women's large purses set in frames. Some of these opened on either side and were folded together to close; others swung in frames and had two lids. The majority were electroplated.

You can remove the lids of cookie jars and use them as flower containers or for other purposes; but why not utilize them as they were originally intended to be used? Naturally you'd want to treat them tenderly and break them out only on special occasions.

Because their use was once so widespread, you'll find that cookie jars often crop up at estate dispersals and auctions, including those country auctions at which many articles frequently bring higher prices than they would in the cities. Numerous antiques shops stock them, and large quantities are often kept in stock by antiques wholesalers, some of which may sell to you if you write them on a letterhead—even a real estate firm's letterhead.

An excellent time, incidentally, to buy cookie jars is between June and the latter part of August, when many antiques shops suffer from a dearth of customers. This is the season to haggle with dealers over prices. Of course, the shops in the summer resort areas may boost prices instead of cutting them in the summer.

Sugar Is Sweet and So Are You

THE respectable dining table of today sports salt and pepper shakers, sometimes in profusion; but the sugar sifter is nowhere to be seen, consigned, alas, to the mists of time.

The terms "shaker" and "sifter" are occasionally used interchangeably, but they are not synonyms. The sugar shaker, used at times instead of a sugar bowl, held sugar for use on the table. It was made in the same general shapes as were salt and pepper shakers, though larger. The sugar sifter, as it is discussed here, was a perforated spoon through whose openings sugar was sifted on certain foods.

Actually, the shaker is akin to the dredgers or muffineers (muffineer is an eighteenth-century name for spice dredger) once used for spices, cinnamon in particular. Some date before the eighteenth century. Sugar shakers were plentiful in our grandparents' and our great-grandparents' days. Thousands were made of glass with metal tops, many in patterns of glass that are eminently collectible today. Particularly abundant were shakers of milk-white glass with tops of pewter, tin, silver, plated silver, and other metals.

The heyday of the sugar shaker was in the final quarter of the nineteenth century but it continued to be used rather widely until the First World War.

Early in this century, one could find sugar shakers offered by such companies as Sears Roebuck and other mail-order firms, as well as by wholesalers of jewelry and novelties. A 1907 catalogue of the House of

Quality, Chicago, offered a group of cut glass sugar shakers at wholesale prices ranging from a dollar to $1.70 each.

In addition to glass, the shakers also were made of porcelain and
metal, and some were of the so-called silver overlay glass—glass decor-

Sugar shakers made in the latter part of the nineteenth century. All are silver-
plated except the one in the top row, extreme left (crystal) and the large one in
the center (cut glass). The small glass one originally wholesaled for only $4.00
a dozen. Prices of the others at wholesale ranged from $2.50 to $4.25 each.

ated by electrodeposited silver. Wholesalers offered glass sugar shakers in either clear crystal or colored glass around 1905 for as little as $4.00 a dozen, including silver-plated tops. Occasionally, but not often in print, the shakers were referred to as "dusters." As was the case with

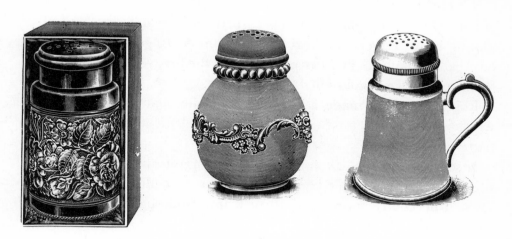

so many glass novelties, ruby, or cranberry, glass was popular with sugar shaker producers.

Although there are not nearly as many sugar shakers around as there are salt and pepper shakers, the former are definitely worth collecting. The earliest you will find easily will probably be of milk glass. These should be worth $7.50 to around $15.00. Colored glass will come higher, choice ones being worth $17.50 to $35.00. The Mt. Washington Glass Company made beautifully decorated sugar shakers in satin glass. These will set you back still more—but are worth it.

Dr. Arthur G. Peterson in *Salt and Salt Shakers* devoted a couple of pages also to sugar bowls and shakers. He disclosed in this that some sugar shakers have been reproduced in several patterns and colors. Watch out for these.

About 1890, the Adelphi Silver Plate Company made an outstanding line of decorated sugar sifters in heavy silver plate, some decorated by repoussé, others embossed. One of the company's catalogues shows a couple of these embossed with figures of cherubs with torches climbing among flower vines. It looked to me as if the cherubs were handling fire pretty carelessly, but I am willing to give them the benefit of the doubt and assume they knew what they were doing. Other shakers were adorned with rather crowded floral decoration. This line ranged in price, at wholesale, from $2.10 to $4.75 each.

Sugar sifters were actually spoons with oversized perforated bowls and fancy handles. Bowls were made in both oval and oblong shapes and were decorated with embossing or engraving. Sifters were made of both sterling and plate and were turned out by many silver and silver-plating firms. Rogers Brothers and William A. Rogers produced them in sizeable quantities in silver plate around the first years of this century. Some bowls were gold-lined.

Rogers Brothers made a sifter in its Columbian pattern that sold wholesale, in 1900, for $12.96 a dozen. Portland also was a familiar pattern.

It seems to me that almost anyone in her right mind ought to collect sugar tongs, but I don't know anyone who specializes in these handsome little contrivances, used to pick up lump sugar. Some of these

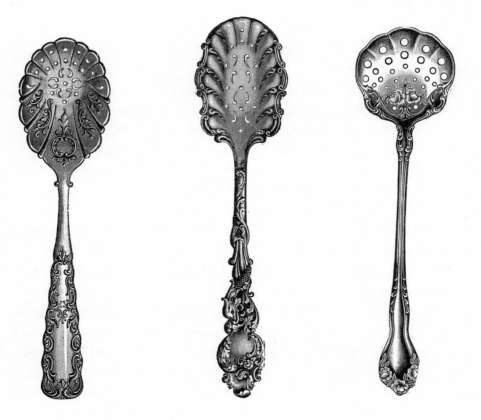

The two sugar sifters at left are silver-plated and the one at right is sterling.

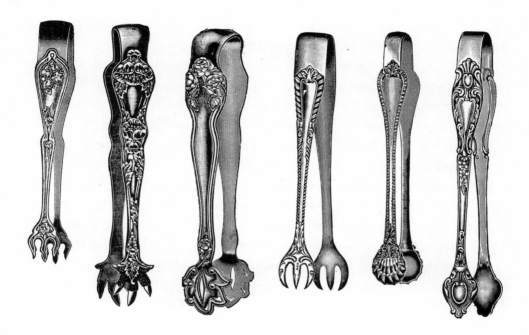

These sugar tongs in intriguing designs were all being offered for sale at the turn of the century. Those on the top row are of sterling silver and those below are silver-plated and were made by Rogers Brothers. The one second from the right on the bottom was advertised in 1892 as the Siren pattern.

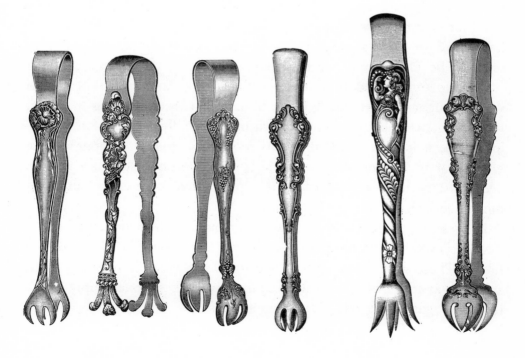

tongs, designed in varied shapes and sizes, ended in three-pronged extremities; others had spoon-shaped ends.

One of the most fascinating I have seen had a cast figure of a cupid, complete with bow and arrow, on the sides. I saw one made in 1892 of sterling adorned on the sides with a female figure who, unfortunately, looked a little pregnant; but perhaps the plump figure merely served to suggest that too much sugar could be fattening. Embossed flowers were often used on the sides of the tongs.

Fancy chased tongs of sterling were selling in 1900 at $2.20 each up to around $4.00, wholesale. Silver-plated ones ranged from around $1.25 to $1.60. One does not see a great many sugar tongs in the antiques shops, even in those selling other silver and silver-plated tableware, but they should sell at prices not much more than those asked for comparable forks, knives, and spoons.

Sugar tongs are no recent invention; they go back to the late seventeenth century. A scissors type was utilized in the mid-eighteenth century. Types quite similar to those made last century date back also to the mid-eighteenth century. Many early ones were produced in pierced patterns. The matching of the tongs with teaspoon patterns dates from the early nineteenth century.

Granulated sugar was preceded by loaf sugar, and sugar cutters were utilized to break these rather hard loaves up. These cutters resembled miniature ice tongs with sharp blades; some had a spring between the handles. Both grocers and housewives once used sugar cutters, but they seem to be exceedingly scarce today.

An implement used to pound the hard sugar into granulated form was the sugar crusher, made of both glass and metal, oblong in shape, with a somewhat knobbed end for crushing. Usually three or four inches in length, it is akin to the drink stirrers in use today. Although these are not of much monetary value, they are interesting and are scarce, because so many were discarded after granulated sugar came into commonplace use.

If these sugar adjuncts interest you, you may also wish to keep a weather eye out for lump or loaf sugar trays, once used on dining tables. These were made of both glass and metal and came in various sizes. Sugar tongs, of course, were utilized with these; one simply didn't lift the sugar cubes out with one's fingers.

Unless you acquire them by inheritance, you'll have to depend on the antiques shops for your supply of sugar shakers; but remember that prices are likely to vary from shop to shop, so hunt around for bargains. The loaf sugar trays often accrue to stores that handle used merchandise. One day before long, collectors are going to "discover" them. Keep on the alert for those with silver or plated handles. They can be used as relish containers on your table, and you will find a number of other uses for them if you will set your mind to it.

Sterling-silver sugar loaf holders, ca. 1918.

On the Level

YOU may think this is going from the sublime to the ridiculous, but, to lapse into the vulgar parlance, it ain't necessarily so. In case you skipped the preceding chapter, the sublime from which we are going is the sugar shaker and other tidbits related to sugar use; and the not necessarily ridiculous field upon which we are entering is that of the level—the device used for so many years to determine whether a surface is horizontal or to adjust something to a horizontal surface.

What you may not know about levels is that they not only are useful devices and have been utilized for many years by carpenters, masons, surveyors, and gunners, but that they also were once quite ornamental devices and that they took many shapes, sizes, and forms.

The best-known level is the so-called spirit level, in which a horizontal line is ascertained through the use of a bubble of air floating in a fluid contained in a small glass tube. Fluids commonly used were alcohol and ether. These devices were combined with mounted telescopes for use in surveying.

Last century, these levels were set in frames of ornamental cast iron (as well as wood), and some of them are true beauties. Probably the reason that they have been thus far ignored by collectors (except perhaps by collectors who specialize in tools) is that all of us have been too busy traveling down the well-worn collecting paths. But one day soon, perhaps shortly after this book appears, levels are going to find

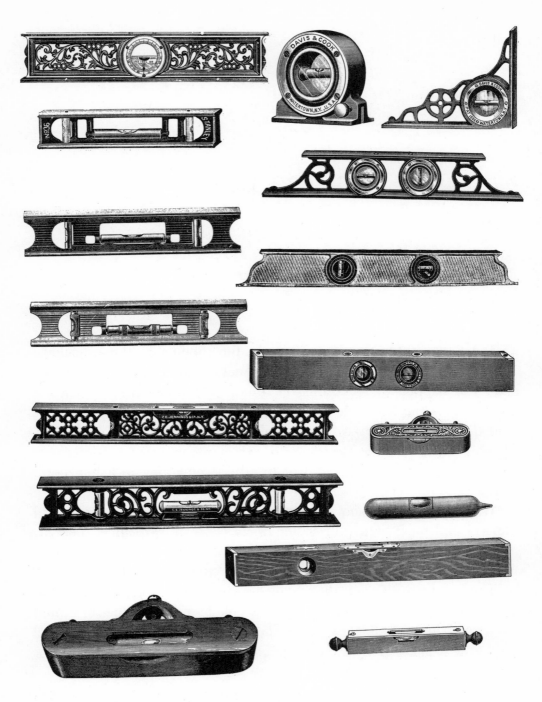

From top to bottom at left are: a japanned machinist's level and inclinometer of iron with adjustable center; three iron plumbs and levels of 1899 with nickel-plated trimmings; two cast-iron levels with pierced decorations made by C. E. Jennings & Company, ca. 1901; and an 1884 Chapin pocket level. From top at right are: two Davis & Cook patent levels (which can be used as plumbs or levels when utilized with a square); three other levels by the same company, all themselves suddenly thrust into the category of collectible objects, and you may find them difficult to locate.

Just as the last century ended, the firm of C. E. Jennings & Company was making a terrific line of ornamental cast-iron levels called double plumbs. These levels had three tubes of fluid with the air bubbles, one of them situated in a horizontal position for use when the level was placed flat on its oblong bottom, and the other two in a vertical position for use when the level was placed on end. It is the ornamented iron, however, that will interest the collector. Other producers of fine ornamental iron levels included the Davis Level and Tool Company, Millers Falls Company, the Cook Company and others.

A large number of combination plumbs and levels were made, and masons could not have worked very well without them. Those with wooden bodies cost about half as much as those of cast iron.

These ornamented iron levels featured scrollwork and die-cut openings that imparted quite a handsome appearance.

Levels ranged in size from about three to thirty inches in length, depending on the purpose for which they were to be used. Some were in the shape of a triangle. Moreover, there were ornamental pocket levels and there were level glasses, the latter consisting solely of the tube without the frame. Cousins of the levels were the inclinometers. These could be used to determine the inclination or dip of the earth's magnetic force by the use of a magnetic needle, and for other purposes that are somewhat beyond my comprehension.

Our ancestors sometimes had peculiar ways of saying things, and some of the large levels were advertised as being packed "one-twelfth dozen in a box."

The wooden levels are far less interesting than the decorated iron ones, but some of the former had metal trim, usually of brass or nickel. If you're going to collect levels, you should have a few of the wooden ones. They were fashioned of cherry, mahogany, and even rosewood.

A lot of persons have begun to collect early tools. The level was certainly a tool of several trades and the early ones should be salvaged.

---

dating around 1901; an iron pocket level (1901); a level glass (1901); a 1901 level with wooden case; and an 1884 Davis patent iron pocket level.

If you'll take the trouble to search through some of the nineteenth-century hardware catalogues, you'll discover in just what great variety levels were once produced. But since the catalogues are scarce and to save you the trouble, we're picturing a number of them here. When collections of old tools are offered for sale, take a good look and see if you can't find a level or two among them. You'll be glad you did.

Top row, from left: Davis patent iron level, plumb, and inclinometer, and a Stanley machinist's level of decorated iron (1889). Second row: two Davis patent iron bench levels and a hexagonal level of 1889. Third row: two Millers Falls Company 1901 patent iron levels, and a Stanley level. Fourth row: another Millers Falls level and a 1901 Stanley pocket level. Below are two 1884 Chapin levels.

Those living in rural areas once did a lot of their own carpentry work, and some of them still do, so that you may find desirable old levels in the tool sheds of country homes. "Pickers"—those roving experts who travel about from community to community, picking up collectors' items from individuals and shopkeepers alike and selling them to antiques dealers—are in an excellent position to look out for these levels. If you know an antiques dealer who buys from pickers (and a good many do), ask him to pass along to his pickers the word that you're interested in unusual levels at a reasonable price.

Pickers may be able to acquire them for a real pittance, passing them along to your dealer for a small profit, and your dealer, in turn, may add only a small profit when he offers them to you.

When you attend auctions, take the time to examine carefully any accumulations of carpenter's tools that may be offered for sale; you may find a collectible level in the lot—and, unless the other tools are rare, you might be able to claim the collection for a small bid.

Porcelain for the Masses

FOR the collector who cannot afford hordes of porcelain plates from Meissen and vases from Sèvres, there's always Carlsbad china. Some of this has much to commend it.

For many years, Carlsbad (sometimes spelled Karlsbad) has been a center of porcelain production, the quality of some of which is a good bit higher than generally assumed. Over a long period large quantities of porcelain were exported from this Czechoslovakian city to the United States, and pieces of it graced many a table in years gone by. Not only did the Carlsbad factories turn out dinner services; they also made toilet sets, vases, cracker jars, miscellaneous bowls, trays, and other items. Both decorated and undecorated, or "white," pieces were made.

Much of the undecorated china was bought by decorators, who hand-painted it and then resold it.

What can be said about Carlsbad porcelain applies to a large extent to many pieces you will encounter with the name Bavaria on them. When the names Carlsbad or Bavaria (or the names of other countries) are found imprinted or incised on porcelain, it is evidence that these pieces were produced after 1891 as a result of a requirement of our tariff legislation.

A fairly large percentage of the porcelain made in Carlsbad factories and imported into the United States was made either in Carlsbad factories owned by American importing firms or was made expressly for them.

For example, you'll encounter many pieces bearing the mark of Bawo & Dotter. This was an importing firm established in New York City during the Civil War. In the early 1870s, this company established the Elite manufactory at Limoges, France, and about a decade later founded a porcelain decorating company in Carlsbad. The latter decorated china made by other companies. The Carlsbad wares imported by Bawo & Dotter are marked on the bottom with a depiction of a lion inside a shield or with a castle beneath a crown, encircled by the words "Bavarian China." Some of this porcelain is of very good quality and is now collectible, though at prices far below those prevailing for productions of the well-known European and English factories of the eighteenth and early nineteenth centuries.

Bawo & Dotter also served as agent for a number of other porcelain manufacturers, among them W. T. Copeland & Sons of England. Moreover, the firm registered other marks for various types of porcelain it sold, including a Silesian mark.

Another New York importing firm whose mark is often found on china is C. L. Dwenger, which frequently used a double circle with the words "Carlsbad Austria" in an outside circle and "A.K.C.D." in an inner circle. Still another New York firm, Heinrichs, used as its mark the words "Karlsbad" and "Austria" and the initials "H&Co." Begin-

Thayer & Chandler of Chicago imported this Bavarian white Derby pattern porcelain in the 1920s for decoration by artists, amateur and professional. A 100-piece set sold for $33.00 to $45.00.

ning collectors sometimes mistake the latter for a Haviland mark, but Haviland wares were not, of course, made in Carlsbad. Lazarus & Rosenfeldt, another New York importer, used the mark "Victoria, Carlsbad, Austria," accompanied by the depiction of an eagle within a circle. The importing firm of Hamburger & Company utilized its initials, "H&G."

Much porcelain made in Austria also carried marks registered by American companies. L. Straus & Sons of New York utilized the name "Rudolstadt," accompanied by a shield and the initials "RW," and other marks, including "L.S.&S. Carlsbad." The name "Leonard" will be found on pieces of Austrian china, which also bear a circle imprint. This was the mark of P. H. Leonard, also of New York.

When you come across wares with any of the marks mentioned above, examine them carefully. Although a great many will not be antiques by legal definition, they are interesting and worth acquiring at the reasonable prices now available.

A considerable quantity of Bavarian china is attracting collectors. Some quite interesting productions were made by the Royal Bayreuth factories, which shipped quantities into the United States between 1891 and 1905, when their operations ceased. Among the Royal Bayreuth creations were numerous novelty items, including pieces in the shapes

This set of Bavarian white china in the Racine pattern (also called Ranson) was offered in the early 1920s to artists who applied white and gold decoration. A 100-piece set was advertised originally at a sale price of only $35.50!

of vegetables, animals, and so on. A Sunbonnet Babies series made in Royal Bayreuth china was patterned upon the Sunbonnet Baby created by Bertha L. Corbett, an artist. The babies were depicted without faces and with oversized bonnets on their heads. The series included cruets, cups and saucers, cream and sugar sets, pin boxes, bowls, and other articles. A Sunbonnet Babies bowl may be worth around $15.00 to $20.00, a pin box about the same, and a cruet, up to around $50.00. Although the factory dates back to the late eighteenth century, the productions that flooded into this country are not yet old enough to be considered antiques. That doesn't mean the collector should pass them by. Their prices almost surely will rise.

Another Bavarian manufacturer was Philip Rosenthal of Selb, whose marks include crossed swords with a crown at the top and the initials "RC" below; crossed swords (or lines) with a crown and the name "Rosenthal," and a fleur-de-lys with attached flowers. This company, established in 1880, created some very fine pieces, particularly in tablewares and in figure models.

Pirkenhammer of Brezova, Bohemia (near Carlsbad), a successor to other early firms, also made top-quality porcelain, adroitly decorated. Lithophane lamps were among its productions. Included in its early marks were the initials "C.F.," "F&M," and "F&R." The name "Pirkenhammer" appears on late productions.

In the 1920s, Thayer & Chandler of Chicago, a firm specializing in artist's supplies and white china for decorators, offered Bavarian "Derby" dinnerware sets. The Chicago company imported the undecorated pieces from various Bavarian manufacturers and sold a breakfast set of fifty pieces of it for $14.50. These pieces were decorated by both professional and amateur artists in this country. Thayer & Chandler also handled another Bavarian line it called "Racine" and offered it for gold and white decoration. The designs were fairly simple, and a set of 100 pieces sold in 1920 for $35.50.

Because these various productions of which we have been writing are, by and large, not yet antique, their prices will fluctuate widely. Not long ago, a ninety-four-piece Heinrichs decorated service for twelve was advertised at a price of only $135.00. To judge values accurately, you'll have to develop a "feel" for quality, and then you'll be able to pick up some bargains whose prices will be enhanced in the coming years.

A line of Bavarian china was marked "Sèvres." Of course this is not the famed china known by the name, which was produced in France. Undoubtedly this name was used by its Bavarian producer to take advantage of the renown of the Sèvres name. Among the other marks you'll find on Bavarian porcelain are such initials as "R.C." with the addition of "Bavaria," "Z.S. & Co. Bavaria," and "R.M. Bavaria."

Some of the porcelain we have written about in this chapter was originally sold by jewelry stores in this country; some was sold at low prices by department and variety stores. But if you want to know what could happen to the prices of some of it in the coming years, just remember what has happened to Carnival glass, much of it nickel-and-dime stuff of not too many years ago.

Thirty Days Hath September...

―――――――――――――――――⊰◇⊱―――――――――――――――――

CALENDARS of one sort or another date back centuries, but the novelty metal calendar frame was the creation of our grandfathers or our great-grandfathers and dates back only to the late nineteenth century.

Desk calendars were just as important in 1895 as they are today, because, like so many of us, our grandparents couldn't remember the day of the week either. Many of our recent ancestors hung calendars on their walls, it's true; but many others preferred them in frames which could be placed neatly upon a writing desk and not only tell the month of the year and day of the week but also lend a certain aura of elegance.

Silver-plated calendar frames, complete with calendars, were made in a host of sizes and styles and more often than not were graced with embossed decoration. Those who preferred gold-plated ones could find these, too.

Quite early in this century, many silver-plated and gold-plated calendar frames bore the name of Wm. Schimper Company, a firm that mass-produced them to sell at retail prices of about $1.50 to $3.00. Some of the silver-plating companies also manufactured them.

Some of these calendar frames were footed and others appeared in clocklike shapes with ornate scrollwork around the edges. Still others were made of white metal.

If you can find calendar pads that will fit in their openings, you can still use these as calendars, but you may prefer to utilize them for photographs instead.

Two ornate turn-of-the-century calendar frames (top left and bottom right), the upper one silver-plated and the lower one in gold plate; and two gold-plated photo frames typical of the late nineteenth century.

Late nineteenth-century photograph frames, all gold-plated and hand-burnished. The tripod stand at left took a picture two by three inches in size and originally sold for $4.00 a dozen, wholesale. These were made by M. S. Benedict Manufacturing Company.

Contemporaneous with the calendar frames were metal frames designed specifically for photographs and called "cabinet photo" frames. These were made in even more varied shapes than were the calendars. Designed to be placed on the dressing table, a table in the living room, or a desk, these frames—some of them so elaborate as to be gaudy —held photographs of members of the family or friends and sometimes, autographed photos of celebrities. Frames six inches wide and seven inches tall were produced in carload lots, but many preferred those that were oval in shape. The photos, naturally, were placed behind glass in these frames.

Especially interesting are some of the frames made in lacy openwork designs. The cabinet photo frames had a support at the back so they could be placed upright on a flat surface.

Closely kin to the calendar and photo frames were metal mirror frames for both wall and dressing table use. In the production of these, designers and manufacturers reached the zenith in imaginative extravagance. Gold-plated mirror frames were made in some profusion and probably were preferred to those of plated silver.

Early catalogue illustrations show these with cast angels frolicking atop them, with floral ornamentation, or with scrolled legs.

If you'll take a look at some of the illustrations in this chapter, you'll have no doubt that many of these calendar, photo, and mirror frames were fascinating, if not always in the best of taste.

The smaller ones will make excellent display cases for your photographs and can lend a quaint charm to the room in which they are used. Particularly interesting are the calendar and photo frames supported by miniature easels or tripod legs. Around 1905, one silver-plating company produced this type with a glass size two by three inches to wholesale at only $4.00 a dozen.

Why use the starkly plain photo frames of today for your small photographs when so many of these earlier frames are still around and can serve as conversation pieces in your home?

Scores of early picture frames are selling like hot cakes today, and it's high time someone investigated the frame types with which this brief chapter has been concerned. Many of them are still in use in older homes, and it is not at all inconceivable that they have gravitated in some numbers to the junk shops and secondhand establishments.

For Muddy Shoes

THE footscraper is a simple but serviceable device which once performed yeoman duty for the nineteenth-century homemaker who was constantly harassed by muddy tracks on her floors and carpets.

Footscrapers were once widely used for precisely the purpose their name indicates, and they saved both carpets and tempers in years gone by.

The footscraper of the 1880s was neither ignoble nor inconsequential, although it was simply made, usually of japanned iron. Certainly it can hold its head higher than a doormat, which is a dreary-looking affair, even when lettered hopefully with the word "Welcome." The doormat lacks character; the footscraper boasts of it.

The footscraper had its heyday before the widespread advent of paved streets and sidewalks. It stood proudly and cheerfully at the entrance to homes, inviting occupants and visitors alike to scrape the dirt and mud off their boots or shoes before entering the neatly swept house. On rainy days in particular it was little short of a godsend.

But in this day, when paved streets and sidewalks are almost universal except in the hinterlands, the footscraper has about disappeared and the insipid doormat has taken its place. Although there was some variance in their size, the average footscraper of the late nineteenth century measured about seven inches long and six and a half inches tall. Some were fairly plain contrivances, but others were so intriguingly contrived and presented so fascinating an appearance that it is difficult to understand why we did not persuade them to survive and grace our entranceways, sidewalks notwithstanding.

The footscraper consisted essentially of a base, which could be attached to a wooden floor or stoop or could be set into stone, and a thin horizontal iron bar upon whose top edge the boot or shoe could be scraped clean of debris. The scraping bar was often held by ornamental iron end pieces and rested upon a scrolled iron piece with cut-out or pierced decorations and which, in turn, was attached to the oval or rectangular iron base.

If you will take a look at the illustrations, you will see just how delightful a footscraper can be.

Footscrapers were made by various foundries that also produced a variety of other cast-iron pieces, and they were originally so inexpensive that even the poverty-stricken could afford the simpler ones, wholesaling for as little as $.95 a dozen! Even the ornate types that could be set into stone were wholesaling in 1884 at only $2.20 a dozen.

The suburbanite who is lucky enough to have a yard and perhaps even a tiny garden patch will find the footscraper very handy after working outdoors. There is no reason to limit the footscraper to the front entrance to the home; one at every entrance would be a boon.

But if you want to be stubborn and continue using doormats, you can display a collection of ornamental footscrapers upon a shelf or along a wall inside the house.

You can still find these charming old footscrapers on the porches of some Victorian homes or even those of a bit later date that have survived the encroachment of apartments and office buildings. If you will visit the yards of the various wrecking companies in your community, you may find a footscraper or two; and if you will let the operators of these establishments know that you are interested, they probably will save the footscrapers they come across when wrecking old homes to make way for what we call progress. Stop, too, when you come across an old residence that is being torn down and investigate to see whether a footscraper may lie within your reach. If so, you can probably bargain for it on the spot, and it is not likely to cost you more than a dollar or two.

By and large, footscrapers do not seem to have gravitated to antiques shops as yet, so the salvage yard offers you the best promise of reward.

These footscrapers date from the last quarter of the last century. The one at left in the second row from the top was designed to be set in stone, with a hole drilled through the base, into which lead could be poured.

With erstwhile farmlands being taken over so rapidly for suburban residential subdivisions dotted with genuine houses complete with yard, the forgotten footscraper could rise again to a position of some eminence and of meritorious service. Businessmen whose incomes have enabled them to attain the status of country squires ought to be interested and should provide a market for those you may acquire. Provided, of course, you can bring yourself to part with them.

I acquired my own ornamental footscraper from a salvage yard at the cost of a dollar and a half, and it now graces the entrance to the room that houses my art glass and paperweights. If you'd like to buy it, it will cost you $25.00, which I think is a fair price and will give you some indication of the profit you can make by tracking down these objects from a past generation.

Trinkets and Treasures

LADIES of the late Victorian era were captivated by trinkets. In their homes and outside them, they were the prisoners of trifles that ranged from jewelry of paste and semiprecious stones to barrettes set with imitation gems. As they cluttered their parlors with multistyled furniture, bric-a-brac, and Rogers Groups, so they crammed their dressing rooms or boudoirs as well as their persons with glittering baubles and tiny treasures.

To serve as repositories for this miscellany of minutiae, manufacturers provided a great variety of boxes and trays. The latter—whether they were intended to hold pins, combs, or rings—have been lumped together through the years under the generic name trinket trays.

Trinket tray collecting offers opportunities for those who must keep the reins constantly checked on their budgets for collectibles. These trays not only are around in some abundance, but many of them are available at quite reasonable prices. Moreover, one may assemble a collection of several dozen without duplication.

The majority of trinket trays produced during the past ninety years were plated, although milk glass trays, too, were made in abundance. Lesser but nevertheless substantial quantities were made of pottery, porcelain, other types of glass, and white metal.

"Pin" trays were specifically designed to hold hairpins, and a surprisingly large number of these were lettered with the phrase "A

Woman's Friend." Tray borders were scrolled or beaded, and a large percentage of the trays stood on small ball or bun feet.

Trinket tray shapes in the eighteen-nineties and early nineteen-hundreds ranged from rectangular to bizarre. Some resembled oversized flower petals or leaves. Heads of ladies with flowers in their flowing locks were embossed on some plated trays and on others formed a part of the border design. One dazzling tray was graced with a female figure with bare breasts and three butterfly-like wings lying on the bank of a pool and gazing into her languid reflection in the mildly rippling waters. The entire surface of some trays was covered with embossed flowers, leaves, vines, or other pictorial representations.

Plated trinket trays should be acquired only if their coating of original silver remains in relatively good condition; replating would cost more than most of these articles are worth. At the opening of this century, plated trays sold at prices of from about $1.50 to $3.00. Many are now available at prices of $2.00 to $7.50, and elaborate plated trays can be found for around $10.00 or so. You may have to pay more for these inexpensive trays when purchased in homes rather than in shops. The reason is that dealers know their values, but owners, who have probably inherited them, add a cash sentimental value to their prices.

Trinket trays of milk glass, usually oblong in shape, will quite frequently be found with their embossed decorations touched up with gold leaf, or, worse luck, a rather sickly green paint. If the gold is in good condition, you probably will wish to leave it. The green paint remnants can be removed with almost any type of paint remover. The average antiques shop will usually have a few inexpensive milk glass trays, whose prices will range from $3.00 or $4.00 to $15.00 or thereabouts, depending on size, age, and scarcity. In addition to white milk glass, a limited number were produced in green and blue, either of which is likely to cost you more than the white.

The milk glass trinket or dresser trays were made in shapes as numerous as those in which the plated ones were manufactured and their decorations include even faces of monkeys at the corners. A choice one in the "Actress" pattern is decorated with a woman's head in its center, and it may cost as much as $15.00 to $20.00. You can occasionally find a choice milk glass tray in the "Lady and Fan" pattern for about the same price. This one, though not illustrated here, alas, has a lady with bare breasts reclining along the edge of a huge fan. It would not be considered risqué today perhaps, but it probably was when it first appeared in the Victorian era.

Trays in milk glass are often advertised for sale at reasonable prices in *The Antique Trader* and some of the other collector periodicals. Some dealers specialize in them and have printed price and descriptive lists available.

Pin or trinket trays in hand-painted porcelain were usually decorated with flowers (the rose was *the* popular flower) and gold trimmings.

Four of the silver-plated pin and trinket trays on the top two rows bear rococo decorations and were made by the Adelphi Silver Plate Company late last century. The rose-decorated tray at the right is in porcelain and dates from 1907. The other trays shown were produced variously between the 1890s and 1907. Another porcelain tray is shown at right in the bottom row.

They encountered great demand in the first quarter of this century. Their values should be based on the quality of both the porcelain and the decoration, but they are still fairly plentiful today at prices of $5.00 to $10.00. Since there seems to be a vogue developing now for top-quality hand-painted porcelain, prices of the trays in this category are probably going to rise before long. On the other hand, there has not been any sizable upsurge in prices recently of either the plated or milk glass pieces.

Trinket boxes were made in as great profusion as were trays and they were intended for the same types of trifles as the trays. These, too, were made of plated silver (as well as sterling), milk glass, pottery and porcelain, and Wave Crest ware.

Tops of the metal trays were often hinged to the bottoms, though this was rarely the case with those of glass or porcelain except in the case of the Wave Crest pieces. Trinket boxes in cut glass appear to be rare.

A good many trinket boxes were produced last century in the various factories in Limoges, France. Since the name Limoges carries prestige among today's collectors (not invariably deserved, it should be emphasized), the prices of such boxes with the mark of a Limoges potter are usually higher than those that are unmarked or bear the mark of potteries not yet well known. For example, you may find a nicely decorated but unmarked porcelain trinket box priced at $5.00 to $7.50, but a similar one bearing a Limoges mark would probably cost you $10.00 to $15.00. So whether you buy the marked or the unmarked box will depend on whether you are buying for your personal collection or for eventual resale. It's a pity, but a fact of business life, that favorably known names bear premium price tags.

Although the terms "trinket boxes" and "jewel boxes" were sometimes used interchangeably, the latter were usually larger and more elaborate. As a result, their values are higher.

Apparently jewel boxes plated on white metal were turned out by the carload during the first two decades of this century. These customarily stood on small legs and were embossed with flowers or scrolls. Some were plated with silver, others with gold, and they were invariably lined inside with colored velvet, silk, or a similar material. The majority of these had hinged tops. Just before the First World

War, they sold in department stores, jewelry shops, and assorted emporia at prices of from $3.00 to about $10.00. This type of box seems most popular with antiques dealers who are just starting in business on a limited budget. They can be found in such shops priced at $7.50 to $15.00. Here, again, try to find pieces whose original silver or ormolu-type coating is in good condition. You'll find some caked with grime that can be removed to expose a surface that can be nicely polished with a silver paste. If the interior lining is soiled, you can rip it out and put a new bright lining in.

Far more desirable than the white metal jewel boxes are more elaborate types with a heavier coating of silver that were designed and produced in the eighteen-eighties and eighteen-nineties by numerous silver-plating firms. Quite intriguing, too, and higher in price are jewel boxes of Venetian glass mounted in twenty-four-karat gold plate. They are also much scarcer. Some of this type may cost you $25.00 to $50.00—far above their original selling prices; but they are likely to appreciate in value more rapidly than the cheaper metal ones. Wave Crest jewel boxes are fetching $55.00 to $90.00 with tops and $35.00 and up without tops. They were originally made both ways.

Because of the higher prices of the glass and superior metal jewel boxes and because of their current popularity, your best buys will probably be the boxes plated on white metal. Some interest in these is now beginning to develop; and while you are not likely to make a fortune on them, you may be able to double your investment within five years or less. This type, by the way, is beginning to turn up at outdoor flea markets, where you may often make good buys.

Watch the want ads in your hometown newspapers for the flea markets, held during the spring, summer, and fall months. Those who scan the want ad columns daily can profit handsomely by this little exercise that can be performed over a morning cup of coffee. Incidentally, in the larger cities the "bulldog" editions of the Sunday papers are available either late Saturday afternoon or early Saturday night. Many of my collecting friends buy these papers when they reach the streets, scan the want ads and do not wait until Sunday morning to phone or visit individuals advertising antiques and other potentially collectible objects for sale. When a home sale is advertised for specific hours on Sunday, it is not quite cricket to jump the gun and go calling on Saturday nights; but antique collectors do not always play by the rules. Sometimes they are rebuffed, it's true; but more frequently they're admitted, even if somewhat grudgingly, thereby getting the jump on their fellow collectors and dealers.

The Pot Called the Kettle...

KETTLES not only were among the earliest household adjuncts brought to our shores by the pioneer settlers; they were among the earliest fashioned in this then-new land.

Although the words "kettle" and "pot" are often used to designate the same article, there is a difference between the two technically. As Clarence T. Hubbard pointed out in an article, "The Indispensable Iron Kettle," in the September 1968 issue of *The Antiques Journal,* the early kettles were used primarily to boil meat in; the early pots were utilized chiefly for broths fed to children. And the kettles and pots were considered among the most valuable possessions of our Pilgrims. In addition to the uses just mentioned, these vessels were used to boil clothes in, to make huge supplies of fish chowder, and to boil sea water in so that a residue of salt might be extracted.

Mr. Hubbard, who dug back a far piece to obtain the data for his informative article, reports that the first known kettle in this new country was cast by one Joseph Jenks at Saugus, Massachusetts, in 1642. Subsequently they were cast in various sizes by "country founders," each of whom turned out sufficient kettles to satisfy the demands of his own community.

Early kettles also were pressed into service for boiling maple sap and were used on whaling vessels to extract oil by boiling whale blubber.

Later many kettles and pots were made in iron works that sprang up here and there around the country. Mr. Hubbard reports that one of the earliest of these works was operated by Thomas Hudson in Lynn, Massachusetts, in 1639. And he throws in the intriguing information that pots and kettles were even used in the seventeenth century and later for clearing roads and paths of snow (they were attached to the rear of sleighs to break runner tracks—a procedure he says was known as "kettlin' the roads").

So much for the historical aspect of our early iron kettles and pots. Suffice it to say that their use continued through not only the years but the centuries. Even in the early years of this century, the woman of the house could hardly get along without a big iron pot in which

Cast-iron kettle marked with the name Ellis Griffeth. This could be hung from a fireplace crane or trammel or set in hot coals. (From the collection of Old Sturbridge Village, Sturbridge, Massachusetts.)

to boil her wash. Interestingly enough, our late nineteenth-century pots and kettles are now classified as "primitives" and they are beginning to be collected. You are not at all likely to find many seventeenth- or even eighteenth-century kettles around.

Wash kettles and sugar kettles were known as "country hollowware" late last century. They stood on three legs and were made both with and without bales. There are a lot of these around today, and they are being stocked by shops specializing in primitives. They are selling there at prices of from $8.00 or $9.00 to $15.00 and $20.00 and the huge ones cost even more, as do those of brass. Unless you just don't like to gallivant about, however, you may be able to pick them up much more cheaply by driving out into the countryside and visiting old farmhouses, where a lot of them are still around, usually stored in an outbuilding but sometimes in plain sight in the backyard. Don't forget, however, that most families today in even the remote sections

Cast-iron stewpot with handle and three legs. This was set in hot coals in an open fireplace. (From the collection of Old Sturbridge Village, Sturbridge, Massachusetts.)

are well aware of what you city slickers are buying. You are not likely to be accorded an affectionate welcome if you offer a dollar for a pot that is worth ten to fifteen times that. Still, if you start off with $5.00, you are likely to reach a financial agreement that will be to your advantage. Not many rural families use the pots any more; they press their store-bought washing machines into service.

Pots and kettles were made in many sizes and also in many shapes. Some were used to hang on cranes in the big fireplaces of our earlier homes, and they may be recognized by their flat bottoms. Later ones were made so they could fit into the hole atop cooking stoves. The earlier hand-wrought kettles and pots were irregular in shape; those with neat shapes are later. Those made of cast iron show a line where they were joined.

There is usually one more difference between pots and kettles in addition to the difference in use for the earliest ones mentioned by Mr. Hubbard: the pots bulged out at the sides; the kettles' sides were straight.

The smaller of the nineteenth-century pots and kettles can lend a nostalgic charm to today's fireplaces. You can also use them as planters. Those that have stood out in the weather for a long time are apt to be rusted. The simplest way to overcome this drawback is to paint the pots with a black enamel.

Smaller brass pots and kettles are worth a good bit more than the iron ones of comparable period. A medium-sized pot in brass with a bail is worth $30.00 to $45.00. Begrimed ones can be restored to sparkling condition with a good brass cleaner and polish. Brass pots that are dented are sold at somewhat lower prices, but unless you're pretty good at tinkering, you may end up by making more dents than you take out. Don't forget the copper pots if you find any reasonably priced.

Now beginning to be collected are nineteenth-century wrought-iron and steel stove pans and pots of various kind, skillets (especially the earlier ones with long handles), waffle irons, and allied adjuncts of the kitchen of slightly less than a century ago.

Here are some iron and steel kitchen accessories to watch out for, because they will soon be sought with some avidity by the increasing number of collectors turning to nineteenth-century "primitives" and will be selling for prices well above what they now bring: muffin and cake pans; broilers; griddles; sauce pans (with porcelain liners) ; roasters and bakers. Just starting to show up in some shops are copper wash boilers, selling for $35.00 and up (in 1890 they sold for $5.00 to $10.00 each).

Often you may find these miscellaneous iron, steel, copper, and brass articles in salvage yards, and they show up at country sales. Even late nineteenth-century teakettles made of brass or sheet copper, nickel-plated, could prove a good investment. You can sometimes find these in the salvage yards for a few dollars, and if you want to hold on to them for a few years, your investment will likely have appreciated more rapidly than your stocks and bonds.

Fads in collecting develop suddenly. Look at what has happened to canning jars, telephone and telegraph insulators, whiskey bottles, and trivets. Most of these objects soared into the collector's ken as a result of books or booklets that were published in the past few years. Their authors did a bit of research, assembled photographs or other illustrations, and published their findings or had them published. A flutter of magazine articles can do the same thing for all sorts of gadgets.

Another example is the sad iron. Outmoded years ago by the electric iron, the sad iron found itself an object of utter neglect until somebody figured out how you could convert them into book ends by painting on them with enamel paints. (They also make good door stops.) Five or six years ago on my trips through the countryside, I picked up numerous flatirons at prices of $.25 to $.75. Today, rusted ones will bring $2.50 or more. Exercise your artistic talents on them and you can sell them as book ends for double or triple that. The painting chore will also keep you out of mischief and ease your tensions.

Magnifiers and Readers

A MONG the host of collectible objects used by our more recent forebears that are likely to be "discovered" soon are reading glasses and magnifiers. Of course, these are still being manufactured and used today, but in quantities far less than was the case before the advent of prescription spectacles that virtually eliminate the need for "readers" except in the case of extraordinarily small or faint print or writing or for those who simply will not wear eyeglasses no matter how urgently they may need them.

What will soon catch the attention of the adventurous collector are the handles and the shapes of the early readers and magnifiers. The Victorians of some affluence utilized reading glasses with silver handles, nicely scrolled, or of pearl, while those of more modest means chose magnifiers with handles of silver plate or wood treated to imitate ebony. These were made in all sorts of sizes and shapes, so that those interested in them can assemble a diversified collection with due diligence.

Apparently there has been little research done on magnifying and reading glasses. I had hoped to gain a modicum of knowledge about their origin by reading a two-part article entitled "The Invention of Eyeglasses," by Edward Rosen, originally appearing in 1956 in the *Journal of the History of Medicine;* but after poring over many thousands of words, some fascinating, I learned only that eyeglasses were invented by the Italians and not by Roger Bacon as some have claimed.

Nevertheless, reading glasses have been used for many years, and magnifying glasses are brought out today when one must engage in such chores as studying small maps to determine how to get from here to there or reading newspaper want ads set in agate type.

Some of the silver and silver-plated handles one finds on late nineteenth-century magnifying glasses are identical with those found on manicure accessories, toothbrushes, and other articles of the same period and undoubtedly for the reason that they were produced by the same silver-plating companies.

For the collector there are the round reading glasses encased in nickel rims, oblong readers, folding pocket magnifiers with one, two,

Top row, from left: a seed microscope of brass, lacquered; a combination microscope; and a tripod microscope. Second row: two brass Coddingtons, and a linen tester. At left below is a pocket focusing glass. Next are two aplanatic magnifiers designed for the use of physicians, botanists, and scientists. To the right is an achromatic triple magnifier and below is a reducing glass.

or three lenses housed in nickel-plated cases, magnifiers on tripod legs, pocket focusing glasses with attached rings that could be fastened to key chains, lenses housed in barrel-shaped plated tubes, folding magnifiers with metal spring covers, triplet magnifiers composed of a crown and two flint glass lenses cemented together and providing an image similar to that given by a compound microscope, and other types.

In addition to those made for home use, there are available various special-purpose magnifiers for the use of physicians, botanists, and scientists. Of interest are the tripod microscopes housed in lacquered cut-brass frames and the aplanatic magnifiers designed for use by physicians and that give a perfectly flat field of great brilliance and fine definition.

Inexpensive loupe magnifiers that folded into hard rubber cases were made in the last quarter of the preceding century, and the smallest of these wholesaled for only $8.00 a dozen with a single lens.

Here are objects, then, that have not yet gravitated to the antiques shops, but with the collecting of which one can have a perfectly delightful and perhaps profitable time, for in its own way the early magnifier or reading glass is just as interesting as the snuffbox, the mechanical bank, and the match safe.

You may have to search the by-paths and the hedgerows to find these objects, since, if collectors exist at all, they certainly are not vocal. Watch out for stocks of jewelry stores that are being liquidated, for there is a good chance that you may find some there. Ask about magnifying glasses when you attend house sales; they may be available but they will not be among the articles displayed for sale.

Here is a case, too, in which you can probably set your own price, because no standard values have yet been established. You should be able to buy many of the more inexpensive types for a dollar or two; those with silver or pearl handles are naturally worth more; so are those in brass housings.

If you begin now, you can be the first person on your block to start a collection of reading glasses—and you'll also find they'll help you decipher that illegible handwriting of some of your friends and relatives.

Shades and Lamps

SINCE the Tiffany craze started some years ago, the prices of genuine L. C. Tiffany shades for lamps—large, medium, and small —have soared beyond the grasp of most of us. The price escalation has been similar to that in Carnival glass, with the demand beginning to outstrip the supply.

What you'll have to settle for, then, is a "Tiffany-type" shade; and if you believe some dealers, almost any leaded shade or shade of mottled or slag-type glass is a Tiffany-type shade. This isn't true. The Tiffany shades are something special. They fairly bristle with the man's creative ingenuity. The first Tiffany lamps were placed on sale in 1895, and thereafter a great diversity of types were produced. Those who know Tiffany glass would never mistake any of the hundreds of thousands of other lamps made in Art Nouveau forms and with slag glass shades for them. Yet these expensive imitations were also popular in their heyday, and they are now beginning to ride high again, tugging hard at the coattails of the Louis Comfort Tiffany boom.

Now, there is absolutely nothing wrong with buying the table lamps with shades made of what were once called "Cathedral glass" panels held in place by strips of lead. In fact, some of them are attractive and give a nice diffused light. Just don't buy them under the impression that they're in the class with Tiffany lamps.

Until a few years ago these lamps were what is known as a drug on the market, their going prices, $5.00 to $20.00, which was less than their original selling price in the nineteen-twenties, when they fetched $25.00 to $50.00 in the shops. Today, they are worth $45.00 to $75.00 and more.

The less expensive types had white-metal bases painted a Roman gold to imitate bronze. Their height ranged generally from about twenty-one to twenty-five and twenty-six inches, and most of them accommodated two light bulbs, which were turned on either with a pull chain or a turn button.

Some of these lamps had hand-painted glass shades, often featuring outdoor scenery, and the effects when the bulbs were turned on were not uniformly bad.

These lamps were manufactured by a number of firms that were well known some years ago, several of them located in Meriden, Connecticut. Among these were Bradley & Hubbard, whose productions are often identified by the initials "B&H," and P. J. Handel & Company, which turned out some really charming lamps. It could prove advanta-

These 1924 table lamps had shades described by producers as "Cathedral glass." These were offered as premiums by the Larkin Company for purchase of other of its products or in exchange for its coupons. The highest-priced one is at the upper left, the lowest, at the lower right.

geous for you to watch out for the Handel productions, which are climbing upward in esteem and may one day before long be worth considerably more than their current prices. Another lamp firm with a large output in the nineteen-twenties was the Charles Parker Company, also of Meriden.

Glass lamp shades were also produced by the Helmschmied Manufacturing Company, once located in that popular town of Meriden; R. Williamson and Company of Chicago; Moran & Hastings, also of Chicago; the Macbeth-Evans Glass Company of Pittsburgh; and the Artistic Wrought Iron Works of Cincinnati, among others.

A catalogue of the Macbeth-Evans firm in the author's possession illustrates a group of leaded shades trademarked "Colonial" and "Mission," and a group of metal-encased glass shades called "Cuirass."

Those interested in a more detailed study of the types of lamps and shades produced earlier in this century and the background of companies offering them will find a well-researched discussion in Albert Christian Revi's book *American Art Nouveau Glass*.

One of the periodic revivals of interest in ancient art, which occurred early in this century, stimulated the demand for lamps with "antique" finishes, including bronze bases.

You'll find the lamp bases finished in various colors other than bronze, and these range from brown to copper. They were originally intended to convey the effect of antiquity, complementing that produced by the combination of colored or mottled glass and pierced metal shades.

During the nineteen-twenties, the Larkin Company, Inc., which had been established in 1875 with headquarters in Buffalo, New York, and which at one time had Elbert Hubbard, the well-known author and creative printer, as its promotional and advertising head, offered lamps of the type we have been describing as premiums to those who bought specified dollar amounts of its other products. A lamp with a hand-painted shade and metal base in a copper-bronze finish was offered, for example, as a premium with the purchase of $40.00 worth of the firm's other commodities. The current price for such a lamp today in the shops is $50.00–$100.00, but if you can find one in a private home, you can probably induce its owner to part with it for $20.00 to $35.00, provided you express a casual, not too exuberant interest in it.

As has been the case with most articles of some fragility, these lamps

The table lamp at the top left has a slag glass shade in a filigree metal frame. The shade is twenty inches in diameter. The lamp at right has a shade of decorated slag glass panels. Both date from 1926. Similar smaller table lamps of allied design and from the same period are shown below.

have suffered breakage through the years, and you'll find them offered with one or more panes broken or missing. This does not mean they are an irretrievable loss, because there are companies now that will duplicate the broken panes for you. These concerns advertise in most of the collector periodicals. A lamp of this type with one missing pane is worth about half of what it would bring without damage.

Hundreds of other types of lamps were in vogue concurrently with those with leaded-glass shades, but collectors' interest right now is centered on the latter. This vogue may last a long time, and if you can pick up such lamps at "reasonable" prices (between $20.00 and $35.00), your investment is likely to pay some dividends within the next five or six years.

These lamps, along with various other types, are appearing more frequently these days at auctions in the small and medium-sized cities. Try attending such auctions on rainy days, when the crowd is small. I have, and I've been able to buy several leaded-shade lamps during the past year at $15.00 to $35.00.

Here's an additional tip thrown in for good measure:

There is beginning to develop an interest in small chandelier-type lighting fixtures of metal—brass, bronze, and even pot metal—which hold from two to six bulbs. These can be utilized in homes too small to accommodate the baronial chandeliers. Hundreds of these are being removed from residences that are being demolished in all sections of the country and are gravitating to salvage yards, where they can often be purchased at prices of $2.50 to $5.00. They are already bringing two to three times that in the small antiques shops. These are still plentiful —but they may not be a decade from now.

It's Fun to Spoon

THOSE who collect glass and even metal spooners have a lot of company. Spooners—which is a coined word for spoon holders —once abounded in pattern glass, and not too many have been reproduced, because, for the most part, these vessels that once adorned the table and held just what their name indicates—a supply of spoons —are not costly.

If, however, you'd prefer less company, take a fling at collecting spoon trays. They served exactly the same purpose as the taller and usually round spoon holders, but most of the trays came into use a bit later.

Spoon trays were also made in glass and metal, and they were used not only to grace residential tables but also in restaurants and the dining rooms of hotels.

Apparently, not many spoon trays were made prior to 1900; at least I have not been able to find them in trade catalogues. They came into popularity around the turn of this century, although they by no means replaced the upright spoon holders, whose use continued right on through the First World War.

Pressed glass spoon trays also seem scarce, though some silver deposit trays were produced. On the other hand, some lovely spoon trays were made of cut glass around the close of the Brilliant Period in 1905 and later.

Nearly all the metal (usually silver-plated) spoon trays had a handle at each end or in the center. Some boasted pierced work, embossing, and beading. Grapes and garlands were favorite designs for embossed decoration.

Among the major producers of plated spoon trays early in this century were E. G. Webster & Sons and Homan Silver Plate Company, known subsequently as Homan Manufacturing Company, though probably many silver-plating firms made some.

Glass upright spooners have been collected for much longer than those of metal. The latter were produced as integral parts of serving sets that usually included a sugar bowl, creamer and teapot, and sometimes a serving tray. And almost invariably the spooner was an exact replica of the sugar bowl except that it lacked the top.

Also produced and collectible were combination sugar bowl-spoon holders. In these, the spoons were held by metal clips or grooves around the exterior of the sugar bowl. These combinations were made in silver and plated silver.

It is likely that prior to the beginning of this century, trays for sweetmeats, asparagus, and the like also were used to hold spoons. In fact, I have found trays advertised in 1900 as being "for spoons, sweetmeats, etc."

Those who are intrigued by spoon trays will undoubtedly also find of interest loaf sugar baskets and kindred loaf sugar holders and lemon dishes.

The difference in the loaf sugar baskets and loaf sugar "holders" is that the former were in the shape of oblong trays with a flat bottom and the latter had oblong sides that formed a triangle at the bottom so that the sugar cubes could be placed inside with their bases resting against one side of the holder and a part of their length against the other. They could be lifted out easily this way, and with the fingers instead of tongs if one wanted to be uncouth about it.

Lemon dishes, which held sliced lemons for tea, fish, and so on, were oval and had glass liners. They were decorated by various means, including piercing, and some had handles so they could be passed more easily around the table. These dishes were utilized prior to World War I.

Almost no one seems to be collecting either loaf sugar baskets or lemon dishes, so here again are fields you can pioneer.

Spoon trays of Brilliant Period cut glass (1905) are shown in the top row. The cut glass trays in the next two rows were advertised in 1914. The silver-plated spoon holders date from the last quarter of the last century.

You'll find metal spoon holders in a good many shops handling silver-plated table services, and undoubtedly many of these are being offered as sugar bowls without lids. Dealers who view them as sugar bowls

The silver-plated loaf sugar basket and holder at the top were offered in 1914. The one at the left was a product of E. G. Webster & Sons. The lemon dish at the left in the second row was made by Homan Silver Plate Company, as was the lemon dish directly below it. The dish on the right in the second row, dated 1900, was used interchangeably for spoons and sweetmeats. The two lemon dishes on the right in the third row and the pierced-work spoon tray at left in the bottom row were made by Webster. The tray just above this was called a spoon tray in the catalogue but seems to be a spoon holder. An 1884 combination sugar bowl-spoon holder is seen at bottom right. Note the butterfly finial on the bowl.

with lids missing cut the prices on these below what they would be marked if they possessed lids. Since the spoon holders were precisely sugar bowls without lids, this is where you pick up a bargain.

Spoon trays will now be found occasionally in the same types of shops, where you may also find now and then a loaf sugar basket or a lemon dish unidentified as to original purpose.

Pattern glass spooners sell largely in a price range of $4.50 to $10.00 (except for the scarcer ones such as Actress, Baby Face, Bellflower, and certain others, along with some in colored glass), and you should be able to find simple plated spooners for less—probably three or four dollars, and maybe a bit more for those with pierced designs. The loaf sugar holders and lemon dishes should be similarly priced. Some quite elaborate silver-plated spooners, however, could cost you as much as $25.00 with the silver in first-rate condition. When you encounter such a price, this is the cue to turn the tables and argue that the vessel is a sugar bowl with the top missing.

The Bottle Boom

THERE are fads in collecting just as there are in home decoration, dress, and the art of tripping the light fantastic, and no one knows for sure how long they will continue.

The fad for Carnival glass has extended far beyond the life predicted for it by the scoffers, who said it would run its course in a year or two. Emerging now is a fad for creations of the Art Nouveau years (late nineteenth and early twentieth century). It may reach fever pitch within a year.

But the most remarkable fad of all is that for bottles, which began only a few years ago and is reaching the explosive stage. Within the past three years scores of books and pamphlets have been written about almost every conceivable phase of bottle collecting. Bottle collectors' clubs and associations have sprung up all over the country. Bottle seekers undoubtedly have engaged in more widespread excavations in the past few years than have all the archaeologists in Europe or Asia. They have so let their joy run unrestrained that they have left potholes in a great deal of private property, much to the anguish of some property holders.

Until recent years, interest in bottles had centered largely about such things as historic flasks, but today it has extended to virtually every type of bottle, including whiskeys, soda pop, food, patent medicine, cosmetic, mineral water, beer, household, and miscellaneous. And now canning jars have joined the list.

There is absolutely nothing wrong with this. In fact, it has provided fun and profit for thousands who otherwise might be hanging around pool halls and barrooms. And the interest has certainly turned up a tremendous amount of information about bottle makers, many of whose names might otherwise be lost to posterity. It also has provided grist for the presses that turn out newspapers and magazines.

Yet bottle collecting has suddenly taken a strange twist: collectors have turned to amassing brand-new bottles, which fetch far more empty today than they brought filled a scant few months ago.

It all started with the Jim Beam craze. Someone at the James B. Beam Distilling Company, founded in the eighteenth century in Kentucky by Jacob Beam, came up some years ago with the brilliant idea of fashioning bottles in unusual shapes to commemorate anniversaries

This bottle was produced for Jesse Moore & Company, Louisville, Kentucky, in the form of a flask to hold G. H. Moore Old Bourbon and Rye around 1880. Examples are becoming scarce. (Photo courtesy of Betty and Bill Wilson, Santa Rosa, California.)

and for other special purposes. The first of these special bottles appeared in 1953 in a series. A couple of years later, the Beam company issued a special bottle to celebrate its own 160th anniversary.

Since then, unique bottles have been issued, primarily in china but also in glass, to commemorate various events, salute the political parties, and mark anniversaries of states and even private institutions. Specialty bottles have been issued for some of the company's major customers.

These special bottles have appeared in the shape of slot machines, trolley cars, elephants and donkeys, buildings, and so on. Probably the most fantastic shape of all is that of a bottle issued in 1968 to commemorate the eleventh anniversary of *The Antique Trader,* an advertising periodical that is circulated among buyers and sellers of antiques and other collectible objects and that now boasts the largest

These western whiskey bottles are sought by collectors. At left is a J. H. Cutter Old Bourbon bottle, C. P. Moorman Manufacturers, Louisville, Kentucky, dated about 1880. At right is a bottle with initials monogrammed OPS, and labeled "Bourbon Whiskey, from A. P. Hotaling's Old Private Stock, San Francisco," about 1892. (Photo courtesy of Betty and Bill Wilson, Santa Rosa, California.)

circulation of any periodical in this field. The publication appears weekly in tabloid-size newspaper format, and *The Antique Trader* Jim Beam bottle is in the shape of a tabloid newspaper (with extremely legible front-page type), against which leans a copy of the *National Directory of Antique Dealers,* issued by the same company that publishes the tabloid—the Babka Publishing Company of Kewanee, Illinois.

The Antique Trader Jim Beam bottle.

Sale of *The Antique Trader* bottle was limited for the first ninety days after its issuance to the state of Illinois. It sold at liquor stores, filled, for less than $10.00; and yet, within a week after the announcement of its issuance, these bottles were being advertised for sale to collectors at $36.00 each!

The Jim Beam bottles are issued in limited quantities, making them more desirable as collectors' items. Some prices, however, have reached the point of being fantastic. Not long ago, a bottle issued by this company in 1964 to commemorate the centennial of the First National Bank of Chicago was being advertised at $2100.00! Only 106 of these bottles were issued. A special bottle issued for Harolds Club of Reno is offered at $175.00. Prices of $50.00 to $100.00 or more are not uncommon for various other of the Beam bottles.

For a time the James B. Beam Distilling Company reissued some of the bottles it had originally produced in limited quantities, but simultaneous with issuing *The Antique Trader* bottle, the company announced there would be no more reissues. This heartened collectors and provided a "scoop" for *The Antique Trader,* which first announced it.

It is exceedingly difficult to obtain most of the special Jim Beam bottles at liquor stores unless you are a personal friend of the owner. The proprietors of most of these establishments seem to save these bottles for favored customers. I tried about twenty stores in a metropolitan area quite recently and could buy only one Beam bottle of this type. I knew the proprietor of that establishment.

The Beam craze has now gone beyond the collecting of the special bottles: several dealers are offering bottle labels at prices of $1.00 to $3.25 each, and these prices may be up by the time this book gets off the presses.

More recently, other firms have entered the production of special liquor and other types of bottles, apparently destined to catch collectors' eyes and thereby rise in value. About mid-1968, the J. W. Dant Distilling Company announced its new "Americana"—a series of commemorative bottlings of great moments in American history. These bottles, made of glass, also are being produced in restricted quantities. The company said the bottles would be available at retailers only once, on original order. The first historic events commemorated included the Boston Tea Party, the Alamo, Washington at the Delaware River, Patrick Henry,

Van Dunck's Genever Ware & Schmitz yellow amber figural bottle of about 1880 is a desirable collectors' bottle. (Photo courtesy of Betty and Bill Wilson, Santa Rosa, California.)

Bottles such as these, which held a variety of "remedies" and "cures" in the nineteenth century, are now eminently collectible. (Photo courtesy of the Reverend Wayne S. Nordstrom.)

and the duel between Burr and Hamilton. Each of these bottles is dated with a special collectors' indicia.

Clevenger Bros. Glass Works, producers of handmade bottles, recently issued a John F. Kennedy bottle in a limited edition. Almost immediately after the assassinations of Dr. Martin Luther King and Senator Robert Kennedy, commemorative bottles were issued in their honor (as were various other gadgets designed to turn over a quick buck).

Among the latest bottle creations is a "Hippie" bottle, made in porcelain and first appearing late in 1968 at a price of $20.00. In late August, it was announced that special bottles would be issued honoring the Democratic and Republican presidential nominees chosen in the 1968 conventions of these parties.

Numerous types of brand-new figural bottles are being made and, apparently, are being snapped up by collectors at fancy prices. For canning jar collectors, there is a new bottle commemorating the sixty-fifth anniversary of the Kerr self-sealing Mason jar. Another company has announced the appearance of the first in a series of special Masonic flasks.

Collectible Coca-Cola bottles, whose dates range from 1900 to 1920. The two amber bottles in the center were used in the northeastern United States quadrant but not in New England. A few of the old "pop" bottles, such as that on the extreme left, were used by some bottlers for Coca-Cola. (Photo courtesy of The Coca-Cola Company.)

In addition to these bottles, collectors are now engaged in a rather frenzied search for the glass and porcelain insulators that not long ago adorned the country's telephone and telegraph lines. Several books about these have recently made their appearance.

It is difficult to know just how to characterize these fads or to predict how long they will continue. Of course, there is nothing wrong with buying new bottles and recent insulators—as long as you are fully aware of the fact that they are not antiques. And as long as you take into consideration the possibility that one day the bottom may fall out of such a market. I don't say it will. I say only that the possibility should be considered, just as one considers the possibility that the stock he buys today may take a dive tomorrow.

The only way I know to be sure of getting a supply of the Jim Beam and other special liquor bottles is to become an habitué of the liquor stores. Naturally, I cannot in good conscience recommend this. However, current prices of these new bottles vary somewhat from dealer to dealer, and the best way to find the lowest prices is to keep a running check on the advertisements in the various collector periodicals.

Because of the current widespread interest in bottles, a number of good books on the subject are listed in the selected bibliography of this volume.

All Buttered Up

IN earlier days, when butter making was a family chore on the farm and sometimes required fastidious attention, this product of the joint labors of man and beast merited and often obtained a place of honor on the table. This place frequently was for a handsome (and sometimes elaborate) butter dish of sterling or plated silver. Such dishes, virtually always with covers to protect the butter from everything from insects to heat), were made in profusion and variety in the latter part of the last century. The output continued, though in diminishing quantity, into the first couple of decades of the twentieth century.

For some reason, we are not prone today to treat margarine with quite the respect once accorded our homemade butter, turned a golden yellow by the addition in the winter season of a small amount of an extract brewed from dandelion blossoms or carrots and more often than not identified by the initials of the producer or the mark from a butterprint mold. The chaste china or glass butter dishes that occasionally are utilized on today's tables or the rather pip-squeakish butter pats at our plates pale indeed in comparison with the silver and plated dishes of our forebears.

Some of the silver-plated butter dishes of the last quarter of the last century were majestic affairs. A good many were produced as an integral part of tea or coffee services that included such additional pieces as a pot, cream pitcher, sugar holder, and, quite often, a spoon holder.

The Adelphi Silver Plate Company, Meriden Britannia Company,

Fancy silver-plated and covered butter dishes of late last century produced by Adelphi Silver Plate Company. Note the holders for knives on the sides. The butter knife at the extreme right is the 1847 Rogers Brothers brand in the Priscilla Twist pattern and the one adjacent has a pearl handle, sterling silver ferrule, and plated fancy blade, and was made by Landers, Frary & Clark. Both knives were available in 1907.

and others produced butter dishes in remarkable variety. Particularly choice are those made with hanging covers that could be raised and suspended from the top of the frame or handle. In the late nineteenth century, Adelphi was offering elaborately embossed four-piece tea sets of quadruple plate at wholesale prices of around $25.00 to $27.50. The company also advertised that it made kettles, trays, and cake plates to match some of its tea services. The butter dishes alone wholesaled at prices varying from about $4.00 to $7.75.

The butter dishes with hanging covers were usually oval or round, but other types were square or oblong, the majority of them handled and many of them footed.

Not the least fascinating aspect of the butter dishes is the finial that adorns their tops. The finial was made in numerous shapes and sizes, although most commonplace was one resembling a collar button.

The covers were invariably dome-shaped, rising well above the lower compartment to accommodate adequately the pound-sized cake of butter.

Special butter dishes (for use in hotel dining rooms and restaurants) were produced by most silver-plating firms. The majority of these were of plain burnished plated silver, lacking the embossing that characterized such a large percentage of those for home use.

Probably the majority of covers were made separately and were simply removed for use, but some dishes had hinged lids and those with hanging covers were attached by a hook to the top of the bail-type handle, or frame.

Butter was kept chilled by putting small pieces of ice around an inner metal liner of the base, which had drainage holes so that the water could drain into the bottom as the ice melted. Double-wall devices also were used to prevent the ice from coming in direct contact with the cake or round of butter.

Some butter dishes were made with knife rests on one side, which brings up the matter of butter knives, also eminently worth collecting. In addition to the full-size butter knives for use in slicing the butter in the butter dish, there were individual butter spreaders, which were smaller in size, and there also were butter picks. The last-named were made both as two-pronged devices and with a solid or pierced-metal spear as the pick.

Among the more desirable butter knives are those with designs engraved both on the blade and the handle. This decoration customarily featured flowers or vines, although a good many handles were decorated by beading. The blades themselves were designed in a variety of shapes and usually measured from about eleven sixteenths of an inch to an inch in width at the broadest part. The knives, spreaders, and picks were made in both plated and sterling silver. Some had pearl handles, and these seem to be relatively scarce today.

Sterling butter spreaders were available in 1900 at prices of $3.00 and $4.00 and the larger sterling butter knives were priced at about $4.00 to $7.00. They will cost you about triple that now. However, the plated butter knives that sold at the start of the century for $15.00 to around $25.00 a dozen can sometimes be picked up now for a very few dollars each. Quite desirable are the pearl-handled butter knives once turned out by several firms, including Landers, Frary & Clark, at wholesale prices as low as $18.00 a dozen for those with sterling silver ferrules and triple-plated fancy blades.

Both the butter dishes and the knives are most abundant today in antiques shops that buy the contents of estates. However, many of the smaller shops are beginning to lay in stocks of the plated knives (together with other plated tableware), and I have found desirable ones priced at only $2.00 or $3.00 each. Good plated butter dishes are available in a price range of from $12.00 to $18.00. Choice ones will fetch $25.00 or so unless the plate is badly worn.

One used to be able to pick up these tablewares at fairly low prices at estate disposals, but such disposals today attract so much interest and are often so widely advertised that overexuberant bidders run the prices up in many instances beyond usual retail.

Most of the plated silver pieces that crop up from time to time in establishments handling secondhand merchandise are picked over so thoroughly by dealers that not much is left for the individual collector. If your grandmother still uses the old butter dishes and butter spreaders and knives, flattery may get you somewhere. In fact, unless there are other aspirants for these pieces of hers, try buttering up your grandmother.

Better in Baskets

CAKE, no matter how good, just had to taste better when served
from a nineteenth-century silver-plated basket. Cake baskets, along
with so many other silver-plated table pieces of the last century, have
been relatively neglected by collectors thus far, but some excellent buys
will be found in this field.

These baskets were produced primarily by the same silver-plating
firms that turned out the butter dishes described in the preceding
chapter. A few of them have cropped up lately in some shops at
prices comparable with their original cost seventy-five or eighty years
ago—from $5.00 to $15.00. Resilvered baskets of fine design will come
higher.

Cake baskets proved attractive dining table accessories, and they
were indispensable at teas and informal gatherings of friends. It's true
that there were some outlandish designs, our great- and great-great-
grandparents having been enamored of the ornate; but many of the
early baskets available would be considered in good taste today.

Cake baskets differed from cake trays in that the former were almost
always oval or square in shape and stood either on feet or an oval
base, whereas the latter were usually oblong and nearly always were
footed. The baskets also had bail-type handles, and these were designed
in some intriguing shapes with finial-type attachments in the center.
Trays had handles at each end.

A hand-painted cake plate of the early twentieth century is shown with two oblong silver-plated ones below and three oval silver-plated ones from late last century.

Late nineteenth-century cake trays and baskets, all silver-plated. The tray at top left has fancy embossing, as does the basket at bottom left. Note the word "Cake" engraved on the tray at top right. The plain satin basket at right bottom is in excellent taste.

Although most baskets were oval, one encounters now and then one in oblong shape, footed, and bearing a close resemblance to the baskets, except for the handle.

Particularly attractive are cake baskets with pierced-work bail handles or pierced work connecting the feet. Pictorial embossing on the surface of the baskets was likely to take the form of flowers, vines, or leaves. (Some trays were lettered with the single word "Cake.") In general, the decoration of the baskets was similar to that of such other dining adjuncts as sugar bowls, creamers, spoon holders, and butter dishes. The late Victorian fondness for the rococo was abundantly apparent in both the baskets and the trays.

It's interesting to note that the general shapes and designs of the cake plates were all similar from the eighteen-nineties right on up to the First World War.

Hand-painted cake plates came into popularity in the first decade of this century but did not supplant the silver-plated baskets.

In many instances, the manufacturers of the plated baskets and trays may be identified by the names on the bases of these articles.

Chances are that it will not be long before dealers, becoming aware of the desirability of so many early plated wares, will begin offering replated cake baskets in greater abundance and at sharply stepped-up prices. Both the baskets and the trays can be used advantageously by imaginative hostesses for serving hors d'oeuvres at cocktail parties and bridge sessions.

Right now you're likely to locate these baskets in some of the junky-looking antiques shops, heaped together with a lot of other plated wares. But they also are beginning to appear—either in fine condition or newly plated—in some of the better shops. A resilvered basket may cost you $20.00 to $30.00, but you are likely to be able to pick up those that need resilvering or whose coat of silver has worn thin in spots for half those figures or less. The baskets will crop up at small-town flea markets, offered there by housewives determined to clean out what appear to them to be inexpensive leftovers from the cupboards of their mothers and grandmothers.

You can find them in shops in small towns of the South at prices cheaper than they are offered in similar establishments in small towns of the East and New England.

The primary reason for the current low valuations is that through the years the connoisseurs have looked down their noses at plated wares in general. For the most part, they still do. Until the last few years little had been written about plated silver as contrasted with the abundance of books on early sterling and other silver wares and even Sheffield plate. But now some of the collector periodicals are publishing articles about silver-plated tablewares, and a few persons are even writing books about them. This research will have its impact on values sooner or later—perhaps sooner than you think.

A Word of Caution

———————————————⊰◇⊱———————————————

WE started off talking about prices and it seems advisable to close with a word about this same subject.

For several years until 1968 there had been only one general price guide to the broad field of antiques available. For a few years the sale of this guide had been limited to dealers, but it was subsequently made available to the public. Late in 1968, however, two additional general price guides appeared on the market. These, too, are available to anyone who wants to buy them.

Price guides (and prices cited in the book you are now reading) can pose a problem. They are certainly helpful if they are used as guides and are not used by dealers and collectors for the purpose of fixing prices. Dealers in general and advanced collectors know better than to expect that the same price for the same article in the same condition will prevail at all shops.

There is much greater stability in the prices of traditional antiques from the eighteenth, seventeenth, and earlier centuries than there is in those of collectibles from the nineteenth century. But many factors enter into asking prices of collectible objects, not the least important of these being the individual collector's eagerness to buy a specific object and the individual owner's willingness or lack of willingness to sell it. Sometimes the dealer's overhead expenses are a factor in his prices. Some dealers will cut prices if hard-pressed for current cash; others will not. And there are some who pay no attention to current values or approximations of them but mark all their goods at a specific figure above their cost.

Often prices brought at auctions can be grossly misleading. Auction prices are affected by the number of knowledgeable persons in an audience on a particular day. Some auction houses will issue periodic reports only on selected pieces that brought the highest prices.

If you are a beginning collector, you might as well make up your mind that you are occasionally going to pay more for something you want than it is worth. So who doesn't make mistakes? Dealers are not infallible either. Don't let your mistakes discourage you. That "sleeper" is probably just around the corner.

One more thing: beware of dealers who talk to you in "antiquese" instead of English. They are probably trying to overwhelm you with superior knowledge, confuse you, and soften you up for the kill. Anyone who really knows antiques can talk about them in perfectly understandable and simple language.

Yet, with all the traps for the unwary and all the headaches, collecting can be the most fascinating of pursuits. So who minds a headache once in a while?

Selected Bibliography

A GOOD bibliography relating to the majority of collectibles discussed in this book is hard to come by, largely because so many of these articles are just beginning to move into the collector's ken and little or nothing has been previously written about them.

The books and articles listed below by no means constitute an exhaustive bibliography, but they will be helpful to those interested in more information about these newer "antiques." Readers will find files of some of the periodicals listed in the larger public libraries. In some instances, the publishers themselves may be able to supply back issues of their own magazines.

The list of general books should interest individuals just beginning to collect or who are interested primarily in the newer collectibles. We have lumped together in the category of silver and silver-plated wares books and articles that contain discussions of the items treated in several individual chapters of *The Poor Man's Guide to Antique Collecting*.

GENERAL BOOKS

BEDFORD, John. *Looking in Junk Shops*. David McKay Company, Inc., New York.

———— *More Looking in Junk Shops*. David McKay Company, Inc., New York.

COLE, Ann Kilborn. *Antiques: How to Identify, Buy, Sell, Refinish and Care for Them.* Collier Books, New York.

———— *How to Collect the "New Antiques."* David McKay Company, Inc., New York.

DANIEL, Dorothy. *Cut & Engraved Glass, 1771–1905.* M. Barrows and Company, Inc., New York.

DREPPERD, Carl W. *First Reader for Antique Collectors.* Garden City Books, Garden City, New York.

———— *Victorian, the Cinderella of Antiques.* Doubleday & Company, Inc., Garden City, New York.

———— & Marjorie Matthews Smith. *Handbook of Tomorrow's Antiques.* Thomas Y. Crowell Co., New York.

GROTZ, George. *Antiques You Can Decorate With.* Doubleday & Company, Inc., Garden City, New York.

HUTTER, Heribert. *Art Nouveau.* Translated by J. R. Foster. Crown Publishers, Inc., New York.

JENKINS, Dorothy. *A Fortune in the Junk Pile.* Crown Publishers, Inc., New York.

KOVEL, Ralph and Terry. *Know Your Antiques.* Crown Publishers, Inc., New York.

MACDONALD-TAYLOR, Margaret, Editor. *A Dictionary of Marks—Ceramics, Metalwork, Furniture.* Hawthorne Books, Inc., New York.

McCLINTON, Katharine Morrison. *Collecting American Victorian Antiques.* Charles Scribner's Sons, New York.

———— *The Complete Book of Small Antiques Collecting.* Coward-McCann, Inc., New York.

———— *The Complete Book of American Country Antiques.* Coward-McCann, Inc., New York.

MEBANE, John. *The Coming Collecting Boom.* A. S. Barnes & Company, Cranbury, New Jersey.

———— *New Horizons in Collecting.* A. S. Barnes & Company, Cranbury, New Jersey.

———— *Treasure at Home.* A. S. Barnes & Company, Cranbury, New Jersey.

SCOTT, Amoret and Christopher. *Collecting Bygones.* David McKay Company, Inc., New York.

SHULL, Thelma. *Victorian Antiques.* Charles E. Tuttle Company, Inc., Rutland, Vermont.

TOWNE, Morgan. *Treasures in Truck and Trash.* Doubleday & Company, Inc., Garden City, New York.

WARMAN, Edwin G. *9th Antiques and Their Current Prices.* E. G. Warman Publishing Company, Uniontown, Pennsylvania.

SHOEHORNS, HOOKS, AND GLOVE BUTTONERS

BETENSLEY, Bertha L. *Buttonhooks to Trade—to Treasure*. Published by the author, Chicago.

WINNIE, Thelma. "Hooked for the Fun of It," *Western Collector,* August 1968.

NUT DISHES, FRUIT AND BERRY BOWLS

HOGAN, E. P. "Victorian Fancies: Bride's Baskets and Bowls," *Spinning Wheel,* June 1968.

MEBANE, John. "Fruit and Berry Bowls," *Western Collector,* May 1967.

SHULL, Thelma. *Victorian Antiques*. Charles E. Tuttle Company, Inc., Rutland, Vermont.

PICKLE AND OTHER CASTERS

JENKINS, Dorothy. *A Fortune in the Junk Pile*. Crown Publishers, Inc., New York.

McCLINTON, Katharine Morrison. *Collecting American Victorian Antiques*. Charles Scribner's Sons, New York.

——— *The Complete Book of American Country Antiques*. Coward-McCann, Inc., New York.

SHULL, Thelma. *Victorian Antiques*. Charles E. Tuttle Company, Inc., Rutland, Vermont.

SILVER AND SILVER-PLATED WARES

COYSH, A. W. & J. King. *Buying Antiques: A Beginner's Guide to English Antiques*. Frederick A. Praeger, Inc., Publishers, New York.

DREPPERD, Carl W. *Victorian, the Cinderella of Antiques*. Doubleday & Company, Inc., Garden City, New York.

FREEMAN, Larry & Jane Beaumont. *Early American Plated Silver*. Century House, Watkins Glen, New York.

HARTMAN, Urban. *Porcelain & Pottery Marks*. New York.

HUGHES, Bernard and Therle. *Three Centuries of English Domestic Silver, 1500–1820*. Frederick A. Praeger, Inc., Publishers, New York.

JENKINS, Dorothy. *A Fortune in the Junk Pile*. Crown Publishers, Inc., New York.

KOVEL, Ralph and Terry H. *A Directory of American Silver, Pewter and Silver Plate*. Crown Publishers, Inc., New York.

——— *Dictionary of Marks—Pottery and Porcelain*. Crown Publishers, Inc., New York.

McCLINTON, Katharine Morrison. *Collecting American Nineteenth Century Silver*. Charles Scribner's Sons, New York.

PHILLIPS, John Marshall. *American Silver*. Max Parrish & Co., Ltd., London.

STOW, Millicent. *American Silver*. Gramercy Publishing Company, New York.

THORN, C. Jordan. *Handbook of American Silver and Pewter Marks*. Tudor Publishing Company, New York.

——— *Handbook of Old Pottery and Porcelain Marks*. Tudor Publishing Company, New York.

WARDLE, Patricia. *Victorian Silver and Silver-Plate*. Herbert Jenkins, Ltd., London.

BLACKSMITH ACCESSORIES

KAUFFMAN, Henry J. *Early American Ironware, Cast and Wrought*. Charles E. Tuttle Company, Inc., Rutland, Vermont.

SMITH, H. R. Bradley. *Blacksmiths' and Farriers' Tools at Shelburne Museum*. No. 7, Museum Pamphlet Series. The Shelburne Museum, Inc., Shelburne, Vermont.

VICTORY, Rosemary. "Blacksmith Tools," *The Antiques Journal*, January 1967.

WATSON, Alfred. *The Village Blacksmith*. Thomas Y. Crowell Co., New York.

WILSON, Everett B. *Vanishing Americana*. A. S. Barnes & Company, Cranbury, New Jersey.

KNIFE RESTS

BEDFORD, John. *More Looking in Junk Shops*. David McKay Company, Inc., New York.

SCOTT, Amoret and Christopher. *Collecting Bygones*. David McKay Company, Inc., New York.

BOOKMARKS

BAKER, Wilma Sinclair LeVan. *The Silk Pictures of Thomas Stevens.* The Exposition Press, Inc., New York.

——— "Thomas Stevens' Ribbon Pictures," *The Antiques Journal,* December 1962.

MEBANE, John. "Have You Considered Bookmarks?", *Yankee,* January 1967.

SASSCIER, Agnes L. "Bookmarks Useful and Ornamental," *Hobbies,* October 1958.

PINCUSHIONS

ANONYMOUS. "Pincushions as Collectibles," *Spinning Wheel,* November 1955.

LONGMAN, Eleanor D. & Sophy Loch. *Pins and Pincushions.* Longmans, Green & Co., Ltd., London.

WHITTEMORE, Edwin C. "Pins and Pincushions," *Spinning Wheel,* March 1966.

VASES

GROVER, Ray and Lee. *Art Glass Nouveau.* Charles E. Tuttle Company, Inc., Rutland, Vermont.

LEE, Ruth Webb. *Victorian Glass.* Lee Publications, Wellesley Hills, Massachusetts.

——— *Nineteenth Century Art Glass.* M. Barrows & Company, Inc., Publishers, New York.

McKEARIN, Helen and George S. *Two Hundred Years of American Blown Glass.* Crown Publishers, Inc., New York.

REVI, Albert Christian. *American Art Nouveau Glass.* Thomas Nelson & Sons, Camden, New Jersey.

——— *Cut and Engraved Glass.* Thomas Nelson & Sons, Camden, New Jersey.

——— *Nineteenth Century Glass: Its Genesis and Development.* Thomas Nelson & Sons, Camden, New Jersey.

TEA ACCESSORIES

LEWER, H. W. & MacIver Percival. *The Bric-a-Brac Collector*. Dodd, Mead & Company, Inc., New York.

SUGAR SHAKERS AND SIFTERS

HUGHES, G. Bernard. *The Antique Collector's Pocket Book*. Hawthorne Books, Inc., New York.

PETERSON, Dr. Arthur G. *Salt and Salt Shakers*. Washington College Press, Washington, D.C.

BAVARIAN CHINA

COLE, Ann Kilborn. *How to Collect the "New Antiques."* David McKay Company, Inc., New York.

TRINKET TRAYS AND BOXES

BUSSON, Key Russon. "Trinket and Patch Boxes," *Spinning Wheel,* December 1950.

LEWER, H. W. & MacIver Percival. *The Bric-a-Brac Collector*. Dodd, Mead and Company, Inc., New York.

POTS, KETTLES, AND PRIMITIVES

GOULD, Mary Earle. *Antique Tin & Tole Ware, Its History and Romance*. Charles E. Tuttle Company, Inc., Rutland, Vermont.

——— *The Early American House*. Charles E. Tuttle Company, Inc., Rutland, Vermont.

HUBBARD, Clarence T. "The Indispensable Iron Kettle," *The Antiques Journal,* September 1968.

KAUFFMAN, Henry J. *American Copper & Brass*. Thomas Nelson & Sons, Camden, New Jersey.

———— *Early American Ironware, Cast and Wrought.* Charles E. Tuttle Company, Inc., Rutland, Vermont.

LANTZ, Louise K. *Price Guide to Old Kitchenware.* Published by the author, Hydes, Maryland.

McCLINTON, Katharine Morrison. *The Complete Book of American Country Antiques.* Coward-McCann, Inc., New York.

MEBANE, John. *New Horizons in Collecting.* A. S. Barnes & Company, Cranbury, New Jersey.

SLOANE, Eric. *A Museum of Early American Tools.* Wilfred Funk, Inc., New York.

SHADES AND LAMPS

ERICKSON, Eric E. *A Guide to Colored Steuben Glass, 1903–1933; Book Two.* The Lithographic Press, Loveland, Ohio.

FREEMAN, Larry. *New Light on Old Lamps.* Century House, Watkins Glen, New York.

KOCH, Robert. *Louis C. Tiffany, Rebel in Glass.* Crown Publishers, Inc., New York.

REVI, Albert Christian. *American Art Nouveau Glass.* Thomas Nelson & Sons, Camden, New Jersey.

———— "American Art Nouveau Lamps," two-part article in *Spinning Wheel,* March and April 1968.

ROBL, Richard. "American Glass Shades," *Spinning Wheel,* July–August 1968.

SHULL, Thelma. *Victorian Antiques.* Charles E. Tuttle Company, Inc., Rutland, Vermont.

BOTTLES

CEMBURA, Al, & Constance Avery. *1968 Jim Beam Bottles Book.* Privately published and available from Al Cembura, Berkeley, California.

FOUNTAIN, John C. & Donald Colcleaser. *Dictionary of Soda and Mineral Water Bottles.* Ole Empty Bottle House Publishing Company, Aamdor City, California.

KENDRICK, Grace. *The Antique Bottle Collector.* Published by the author, Fallon, Nevada.

————— *The Mouth-Blown Bottle*. Published by the author, Fallon, Nevada.

MAUST, Don, Editor. *Bottle and Glass Handbook*. E. G. Warman Publishing Company, Uniontown, Pennsylvania.

REVI, Albert Christian. *American Pressed Glass & Figure Bottles*. Thomas Nelson & Sons, Camden, New Jersey.

TIBBITTS, John C. *John Doe, Bottle Collector*. Little Glass Shack, Sacramento, California.

————— *1200 Bottles Priced*. Little Glass Shack, Sacramento, California.

WATSON, Richard. *Bitters Bottles*. Thomas Nelson & Sons, Camden, New Jersey.

————— *Supplement to Bitters Bottles*. Thomas Nelson & Sons, Camden, New Jersey.

WILSON, Betty and Bill. *Spirits Bottles of the Old West*. B. & B. Enterprises, Santa Rosa, California.

BUTTER DISHES

HOGAN, E. P. "Silverplated Butter Dishes," *Spinning Wheel*, September 1968.

Index